Python REST API Development

Building and Consuming RESTful APIs with Flask and Django

Thompson Carter

COPYRIGHT

DISCLAIMER

The information provided in this book is for general informational purposes only. All content in this book reflects the author's views and is based on their research, knowledge, and experiences. The author and publisher make no representations or warranties of any kind concerning the completeness, accuracy, reliability, suitability, or availability of the information contained herein.

This book is not intended to be a substitute for professional advice, diagnosis, or treatment. Readers should seek professional advice for any specific concerns or conditions. The author and publisher disclaim any liability or responsibility for any direct, indirect, incidental, or consequential loss or damage arising from the use of the information contained in this book.

The reader is encouraged to consult with qualified professionals before making any decisions or taking any actions based on the content of this book.

Table of Content

Chapter 1

Introduction to RESTful APIs

In the digital landscape today, APIs play a critical role in enabling communication between different software applications. This chapter will provide a comprehensive overview of RESTful APIs, focusing on their significance, fundamental principles, and the tools we will explore in this book, namely Flask and Django.

Definition of APIs and REST

An API, or Application Programming Interface, serves as a set of rules and protocols that allows one software application to communicate with another. It defines the methods and data formats that applications can use to exchange information. APIs are crucial for enabling interoperability among different systems, making it possible for developers to integrate third-party services, data sources, and functionalities into their applications without having to build everything from scratch.

REST, which stands for Representational State Transfer, is a specific architectural style for designing networked applications. RESTful APIs leverage the HTTP protocol for communication, making them web-friendly and easy to use. Unlike other types of APIs, such as SOAP (Simple Object Access Protocol), REST emphasizes simplicity and performance. RESTful APIs represent resources (such as users, products, or orders) and use standard HTTP methods (GET, POST, PUT, DELETE) to perform operations on those resources.

RESTful APIs provide a stateless communication model, which means that each request from the client to the server must contain all the information needed to understand and process the request. This allows for improved scalability and performance, as servers do not need to maintain session information between requests.

Overview of REST Principles

To grasp the concept of RESTful APIs fully, it's essential to understand the guiding principles that define REST architecture. These principles are designed to ensure scalability, simplicity, and modifiability.

One of the core principles of REST is the concept of resources. In REST, everything is considered a resource, and each resource is identified by a unique URI (Uniform Resource Identifier). This allows clients to interact with the resource directly using the provided URI. For instance, a user resource could be accessed via the URI /users/123, where 123 represents a specific user.

Another critical principle of REST is statelessness. As mentioned earlier, each request must contain all the information needed for the server to process it. This means that the server does not store any client context between requests, which enhances the server's scalability and makes it easier to handle high loads.

REST also emphasizes the use of standard HTTP methods. Each method corresponds to a specific action to be performed on the resource. The commonly used methods are:

GET: Retrieves data from the server.
POST: Sends data to the server, often resulting in a new resource being created.
PUT: Updates an existing resource on the server.
DELETE: Removes a resource from the server.

Moreover, REST advocates for a uniform interface, simplifying and decoupling the architecture. This uniformity makes it easier for developers to understand how to interact with the API without needing extensive documentation. This interface can be achieved through standard media types like JSON or XML for representing the resource data.

Finally, RESTful APIs are designed to be cacheable. Caching improves performance by storing responses to requests, allowing future requests for the same resource to be served faster without going back to the server.

Importance of RESTful APIs in Modern Applications

In today's interconnected world, RESTful APIs are vital for building modern web applications, mobile applications, and microservices. They enable developers to create flexible and scalable systems that can communicate seamlessly.

One significant advantage of RESTful APIs is their ability to facilitate integration between disparate systems. For instance, an e-commerce platform can use REST APIs to integrate with payment gateways, inventory management systems, and shipping services. This integration helps businesses streamline their operations and provide a better user experience.

Furthermore, RESTful APIs promote a modular approach to software development. By separating the front-end from the back-end, developers can work on different components independently. For example, a mobile app can communicate with a RESTful API to fetch data without being tightly coupled to the server. This separation of concerns allows for greater flexibility, easier maintenance, and quicker deployment cycles.

RESTful APIs also play a crucial role in enabling third-party developers to access a platform's functionalities. By providing a well-documented API, companies can encourage developers to build applications and services that complement their offerings. This approach not only fosters innovation but also creates new revenue streams.

Another important aspect is that RESTful APIs are inherently scalable. As user demand increases, additional resources can be added to the server without major modifications to the API. This scalability is essential for applications that experience fluctuating traffic, ensuring they remain responsive and performant.

Finally, RESTful APIs are supported by a wide array of tools and frameworks, making them accessible to developers of all skill levels. Popular languages and frameworks such as Flask and Django make it easier to build, test, and deploy RESTful APIs quickly, allowing developers to focus on functionality rather than underlying infrastructure.

Brief Introduction to Flask and Django

Flask and Django are two of the most popular frameworks for building web applications and APIs in Python. Each has its own strengths and weaknesses, making them suitable for different types of projects.

Flask is a micro-framework that is lightweight and easy to use, making it an excellent choice for small to medium-sized applications or for developers who prefer simplicity and flexibility. Flask allows for rapid development and gives developers the freedom to choose their tools and libraries, enabling them to create custom solutions tailored to their needs. Its minimalistic design encourages best practices and promotes clean code.

On the other hand, Django is a high-level web framework that follows the "batteries-included" philosophy. It comes with a rich set of built-in features, including an ORM (Object-Relational Mapping) system, authentication mechanisms, and an admin interface. Django is well-suited for larger applications where rapid development and scalability are critical. Its robust architecture promotes rapid development cycles and provides a solid foundation for building complex web applications.

Both Flask and Django have strong communities and extensive documentation, which means that developers can easily find resources, tutorials, and libraries to support their projects. Throughout this book, we will delve into both frameworks, exploring how to build and consume RESTful APIs effectively.

In summary, RESTful APIs are an essential component of modern software architecture, providing a flexible, scalable, and easy-to-use method for communication between applications. Understanding the principles of REST and how to implement them using frameworks like Flask and Django is crucial for any developer looking to build robust applications. As we progress through this book, we will explore each aspect of RESTful API development in detail, equipping you with the knowledge and skills to create powerful web services.

Chapter 2

Setting Up Your Development Environment

Establishing a solid development environment is crucial for efficient programming, especially when working with RESTful APIs using Flask and Django. This chapter will guide you through the steps to set up your environment, ensuring you have all the necessary tools and configurations in place for a smooth development experience.

Installing Python and Necessary Packages

The first step in setting up your development environment is to ensure that you have Python installed on your machine. Python is a versatile programming language that serves as the foundation for both Flask and Django.

To install Python, visit the official Python website. Download the latest version compatible with your operating system, whether it be Windows, macOS, or Linux. Follow the installation instructions provided for your specific OS.

Once Python is installed, you can verify the installation by opening a terminal or command prompt and typing:

bash
Copy code

```
python --version
```

or

bash
Copy code

```
python3 --version
```

This command will display the version of Python currently installed. It's essential to have Python 3.x, as Python 2 has reached the end of its life and is no longer supported.

Next, you will need to install pip, the package installer for Python. Pip usually comes bundled with Python installations. You can check if pip is installed by typing:

bash
Copy code

```
pip --version
```

If pip is not installed, follow the instructions on the pip installation page.

With Python and pip installed, you can now install Flask and Django. Use the following commands in your terminal:

bash
Copy code

```
pip install Flask
pip install Django
```

These commands will download and install the latest versions of Flask and Django along with their dependencies.

Setting Up Virtual Environments

Using virtual environments is an essential practice in Python development. A virtual environment allows you to create isolated environments for your projects, ensuring that dependencies and packages do not interfere with each other. This is particularly useful when working on multiple projects that may require different library versions.

To create a virtual environment, first ensure that you have the venv module, which is included in Python 3. You can create a virtual environment by executing the following command in your terminal:

bash
Copy code
```
python -m venv myenv
```

Replace myenv with whatever name you wish to give your environment. After executing this command, a new directory will be created, containing a copy of the Python interpreter and a lib directory with the site packages.

To activate your virtual environment, use the following command depending on your operating system:

Windows:
bash
Copy   code
```
myenv\Scripts\activate
```

macOS   **and**   **Linux:**
bash
Copy   code
```
source myenv/bin/activate
```

Once activated, your terminal prompt will change to indicate that you are now operating within the virtual environment. You can then install packages using pip, and they will be confined to this environment.

To deactivate the virtual environment and return to your global Python environment, simply type:

bash
Copy code

```
deactivate
```

Introduction to Flask and Django Installation

With Python and your virtual environment ready, it's time to dive deeper into the installations of Flask and Django.

Flask is lightweight and easy to get started with, making it an excellent choice for those new to API development. To create a basic Flask application, you can follow these simple steps after activating your virtual environment.

First, create a new directory for your Flask project:

bash
Copy code

```
mkdir flask_api
cd flask_api
```

Next, create a new file named app.py:

bash
Copy code
touch app.py

In app.py, add the following code to set up a simple Flask application:

python
Copy code
```python
from flask import Flask

app = Flask(__name__)

@app.route('/')
def home():
return "Hello, Flask!"

if __name__ == '__main__':
app.run(debug=True)
```

You can run the Flask application by executing:

bash
Copy code

```
python app.py
```

Now, open your web browser and navigate to http://127.0.0.1:5000/. You should see the message "Hello, Flask!" displayed.

Django, on the other hand, requires a bit more setup due to its comprehensive nature. To create a new Django project, use the following command:

```bash
Copy code
django-admin startproject myproject
```

Replace myproject with your desired project name. This command will create a new directory containing the necessary files and folders for your Django application.

Next, navigate into your project directory:

```bash
Copy code
cd myproject
```

You can run the development server using:

bash

Copy code
```
python manage.py runserver
```

Django will start its development server, and you can view your application by visiting http://127.0.0.1:8000/ in your browser. You should see a welcome message indicating that your Django project is set up successfully.

Overview of Code Editors and IDEs

Choosing the right code editor or Integrated Development Environment (IDE) is essential for productivity and ease of use. A good code editor can significantly enhance your coding experience, providing features like syntax highlighting, code completion, debugging tools, and version control integration.

Popular code editors for Python development include:

Visual Studio Code: A lightweight, open-source editor from Microsoft that supports numerous extensions for Python, Flask, and Django development. It provides features such as IntelliSense, debugging, and integrated Git support.

PyCharm: A powerful IDE specifically designed for Python development. PyCharm offers robust features such as code analysis, a powerful debugger, and seamless integration with version control systems. While the

19

community edition is free, the professional edition provides additional features for web development.

Atom: An open-source editor created by GitHub that is highly customizable. Atom has a rich ecosystem of plugins and themes, making it a flexible option for Python development.

Sublime Text: A fast and lightweight editor known for its speed and efficiency. Sublime Text supports various plugins and features, making it a popular choice among developers.

When selecting an editor or IDE, consider your workflow, preferences, and the specific features you need for developing RESTful APIs with Flask and Django.

Conclusion

Setting up a proper development environment is a fundamental step toward becoming proficient in building RESTful APIs with Flask and Django. By installing Python, utilizing virtual environments, and selecting the right tools, you can create a streamlined workspace that enhances your productivity and supports efficient development practices.

In the following chapters, we will dive deeper into building and consuming RESTful APIs, leveraging the foundations laid in this chapter. Whether you're starting with Flask or Django, a well-prepared environment will significantly ease your journey into Python REST API development.

Chapter 3

Understanding HTTP Methods and Status Codes

A solid understanding of HTTP methods and status codes is vital for developing and consuming RESTful APIs. These concepts form the backbone of communication between clients and servers. In this chapter, we will explore the various HTTP methods, their usage, and common status codes, ensuring you are equipped with the knowledge necessary to create efficient APIs.

Overview of HTTP Methods

HTTP, or Hypertext Transfer Protocol, is the foundation of data communication on the web. It defines the rules for how messages are formatted and transmitted, and how web servers and browsers should respond to various commands. In the context of RESTful APIs, HTTP methods are used to perform operations on resources, each method serving a specific purpose.

The most common HTTP methods utilized in RESTful APIs include GET, POST, PUT, DELETE, PATCH, and OPTIONS. Understanding when and how to use these methods is essential for creating APIs that adhere to REST principles.

GET

The GET method is used to retrieve data from the server. When a client sends a GET request, it asks the server to send back a representation of a specific resource. This method should not have any side effects; meaning, it should not alter the state of the resource on the server.

For example, a GET request to http://api.example.com/users/123 would retrieve the details of the user with ID 123. GET requests are idempotent, meaning that making the same request multiple times will yield the same result without changing the state of the resource.

POST

The POST method is used to send data to the server, often resulting in the creation of a new resource. When a client submits a POST request, it usually includes a payload containing the data to be processed. This method is commonly used for submitting forms or uploading files.

For example, a POST request to http://api.example.com/users with a JSON body containing user details would create a new user on the server. Unlike GET, POST requests are not idempotent; sending the same request multiple times may result in the creation of multiple resources.

PUT

The PUT method is used to update an existing resource or create a new one if it does not already exist. When a client sends a PUT request, it typically includes the entire resource representation in the request body. This method replaces the current state of the resource with the new data provided.

For instance, a PUT request to http://api.example.com/users/123 with a payload containing updated user details would replace the current user information for the user with ID 123. Like GET, PUT requests are idempotent; sending the same request multiple times will yield the same result.

DELETE

The DELETE method is used to remove a resource from the server. When a client sends a DELETE request, it instructs the server to delete the specified resource.

For example, a DELETE request to http://api.example.com/users/123 would remove the user with ID 123 from the server. DELETE requests are also idempotent, as making the same request multiple times will have the same effect—namely, the resource will be deleted if it exists.

PATCH

The PATCH method is used for partial updates to a resource. Unlike PUT, which requires the entire resource representation, PATCH allows the client to send only the fields that need to be updated. This method is particularly useful for optimizing bandwidth and improving performance.

For instance, a PATCH request to http://api.example.com/users/123 with a JSON body containing only the fields to be updated, such as the user's email address, would update just that field without affecting the rest of the user's data.

OPTIONS

The OPTIONS method is used to describe the communication options for the target resource. This method allows clients to determine which HTTP methods are supported by the server for a specific endpoint.

For example, sending an OPTIONS request to http://api.example.com/users could return information about which methods (GET, POST, etc.) are allowed for that endpoint, helping clients understand how they can interact with the API.

Best Practices for Using HTTP Methods in RESTful APIs

When designing RESTful APIs, adhering to best practices for using HTTP methods is crucial for creating intuitive and predictable interfaces. Here are some key recommendations:

Use the Correct Method for Each Operation: Ensure that you are using the appropriate HTTP method for each action. For example, use GET for data retrieval, POST for creating new resources, PUT for updating existing ones, and DELETE for removing resources.

Be Consistent: Consistency is key in API design. Ensure that the same HTTP methods are used for similar actions across different endpoints. This consistency makes it easier for developers to understand and use your API.

Implement Idempotency: Where applicable, ensure that your API methods are idempotent. This means that clients can safely retry requests without causing unintended side effects. For example, multiple DELETE requests for the same resource should not produce errors after the first deletion.

Handle Errors Gracefully: Implement proper error handling for each HTTP method. Use appropriate status codes and return informative messages to guide clients in troubleshooting issues.

Document Your API: Comprehensive documentation is essential for helping developers understand how to interact with your API. Clearly specify which methods are available for each endpoint and provide examples of requests and responses.

Common HTTP Status Codes

Along with HTTP methods, status codes play a critical role in RESTful APIs by providing feedback about the outcome of a request. These codes are grouped into categories based on their purpose, primarily using the first digit to denote the type of response.

1xx: Informational

These status codes indicate that the request has been received and is being processed. They are rarely used in RESTful APIs.

100 Continue: Indicates that the initial part of the request has been received, and the client can continue with the rest of the request.

2xx: Success

These status codes indicate that the client's request was successfully received, understood, and processed by the server.

200 OK: Indicates that the request was successful, and the server is returning the requested data (for GET requests) or confirming the successful processing of data (for POST or PUT requests).

201 Created: Indicates that a new resource has been successfully created. This status is typically returned in response to a successful POST request.

204 No Content: Indicates that the server successfully processed the request, but there is no content to return (commonly used for DELETE requests).

3xx: Redirection

These status codes indicate that further action is needed to complete the request, usually involving redirection to a different resource.

301 Moved Permanently: Indicates that the requested resource has been permanently moved to a new URL.

302 Found: Indicates that the requested resource resides temporarily at a different URL.

4xx: Client Error

These status codes indicate that the client made an error in the request.

400 Bad Request: Indicates that the server could not understand the request due to malformed syntax.
401 Unauthorized: Indicates that the client must authenticate itself to receive the requested response.
403 Forbidden: Indicates that the server understood the request but refuses to authorize it.
404 Not Found: Indicates that the server cannot find the requested resource.

5xx: Server Error

These status codes indicate that the server failed to fulfill a valid request due to an error on its end.

500 Internal Server Error: Indicates that the server encountered an unexpected condition that prevented it from fulfilling the request.
502 Bad Gateway: Indicates that the server received an invalid response from an upstream server it accessed while attempting to fulfill the request.
503 Service Unavailable: Indicates that the server is currently unable to handle the request due to temporary overload or maintenance.

Best Practices for Using HTTP Status Codes

Properly implementing HTTP status codes in your API responses is crucial for effective communication with clients. Here are some best practices:

Use Appropriate Status Codes: Ensure that you return the correct status code for each request. For example, use 200 for successful GET requests, 201 for successful POST requests that create resources, and 404 for requests for non-existent resources.

Include Additional Information: In addition to status codes, consider including informative error messages in your response body to help clients understand what went wrong. This practice can greatly enhance the user experience.

Avoid Generic Status Codes: Instead of returning a generic 500 status code for all errors, try to provide more specific codes that accurately reflect the issue. This approach allows clients to handle errors more effectively.

Document Status Codes: Clearly document all the status codes your API might return, along with their meanings and potential scenarios. This information is invaluable for developers using your API.

In summary, understanding HTTP methods and status codes is fundamental to effective RESTful API development. By using the correct methods for each operation and returning appropriate status codes, you create a predictable and user-friendly interface for clients to interact with your API. As we continue through this book, we will apply these concepts in practical examples, allowing you to build robust and effective RESTful APIs with Flask and Django.

Chapter 4

Building Your First Flask API

Creating your first RESTful API using Flask is an exciting step into the world of web development. Flask is designed to be simple and flexible, making it an ideal choice for both beginners and experienced developers. In this chapter, we will walk through the process of setting up a basic Flask application and creating a simple API that handles HTTP requests.

Introduction to Flask

Flask is a micro web framework for Python that allows you to build web applications and APIs quickly and easily. It provides the essential tools and functionalities to get started without imposing too much structure, which gives developers the freedom to choose how to organize their code. Flask follows the WSGI (Web Server Gateway Interface) standard, making it compatible with many web servers.

One of the key features of Flask is its lightweight nature. Unlike full-fledged frameworks like Django, Flask does not come with a lot of built-in features, which means you can choose only what you need for your application. This minimalism makes it a great choice for small applications or when you want to quickly prototype ideas.

Setting Up a Basic Flask Application

To start building your first Flask API, you first need to ensure that Flask is installed in your virtual environment. If you haven't done this yet, activate your virtual environment and install Flask using the following command:

bash
Copy code

```
pip install Flask
```

Once Flask is installed, you can create a new directory for your project and a simple Flask application. Here's how to get started:

Create a Project Directory: Create a new directory for your project. You can name it anything you like, such as flask_api.
bash
Copy   code

```
mkdir flask_api
cd flask_api
```

Create the Application File: Inside this directory, create a new file called app.py. This file will contain your Flask application   code.
bash
Copy   code
touch app.py

Write the Basic Flask Application: Open app.py in your favorite text editor or IDE and add the following code:
python
Copy   code

```
from flask import Flask

app = Flask(__name__)

@app.route('/')
def home():
return "Welcome to My First Flask API!"

if __name__ == '__main__':
app.run(debug=True)
```

In this code snippet, you create an instance of the Flask class and define a route for the root URL (/). When a user navigates to this URL, the home function is called, returning a simple welcome message. The debug=True parameter allows you to see detailed error messages and automatically reload the server when you make changes to the code.

Run Your Flask Application: You can now run your Flask application using the following command: bash
Copy   code
python app.py

After executing this command, Flask will start a development server, usually accessible at http://127.0.0.1:5000/. Open this URL in your web browser, and you should see the message "Welcome to My First Flask API!" displayed.

Creating Routes and Handling Requests

Now that you have a basic Flask application running, let's expand it by creating additional routes and handling different HTTP requests. In a RESTful API, routes are defined for different resources, allowing clients to interact with your application.

Defining Additional Routes

In RESTful APIs, each resource typically has its own endpoint. For example, if you were building an API for managing a collection of books, you might have endpoints like /books to list all books and /books/<id> to access a specific book by its ID.

Let's add a couple of routes to your Flask application for managing a simple collection of items.

Modify Your app.py File: Update your app.py to include new routes for handling a collection of items:
python
Copy   code

```python
from flask import Flask, jsonify, request

app = Flask(__name__)

items = [
{"id": 1, "name": "Item 1"},
{"id": 2, "name": "Item 2"},
]

@app.route('/')
def home():
return "Welcome to My First Flask API!"

@app.route('/items', methods=['GET'])
def get_items():
return jsonify(items)
```

```python
@app.route('/items/<int:item_id>', methods=['GET'])
def get_item(item_id):
    item = next((item for item in items if item['id'] ==
item_id), None)
    if item is not None:
        return jsonify(item)
    return jsonify({"error": "Item not found"}), 404


@app.route('/items', methods=['POST'])
def create_item():
    new_item = request.get_json()
    new_item['id'] = len(items) + 1
    items.append(new_item)
    return jsonify(new_item), 201


if __name__ == '__main__':
    app.run(debug=True)
```

Explanation of New Routes

GET /items: This route retrieves a list of all items. The get_items function uses jsonify to convert the items list into a JSON response.

GET /items/<item_id>: This route retrieves a specific item based on its ID. The get_item function uses Python's next function to find the item in the items list. If the item exists, it returns it; otherwise, it returns a 404 error with a message.

POST /items: This route allows clients to create a new item. The create_item function retrieves the JSON data from the request body using request.get_json(), assigns a new ID, and adds the item to the items list. It then returns the newly created item along with a 201 status code.

Testing Your API

With the new routes defined, it's time to test your API using a tool like Postman or Curl. Here's how you can test each of the routes:

GET /items: Use a GET request to retrieve the list of items. You should receive a response containing all the items in JSON format.

GET /items/1: Use a GET request to retrieve the item with ID 1. The response should return the corresponding item.

POST /items: To create a new item, use a POST request to /items. In the request body, send a JSON object representing the new item. For example: json
Copy   code

```
{
"name": "Item 3"
}
```

38

The response should return the newly created item, including its ID.

Returning JSON Responses

One of the primary advantages of RESTful APIs is their ability to return data in JSON format. Flask provides the jsonify function, which converts Python dictionaries and lists into JSON responses effortlessly.

When designing your API, it's essential to ensure that all responses are properly formatted as JSON. This consistency improves usability and enables clients to parse the responses easily.

For instance, when returning a list of items or a specific item, always use jsonify:

```python
Copy code
return jsonify(items)  # For returning all items
return jsonify(item)   # For returning a specific item
```

Using jsonify automatically sets the Content-Type header to application/json, informing clients that the response body is in JSON format.

Error Handling

A well-designed API should gracefully handle errors and provide meaningful feedback to clients. In the previous code snippets, we already included basic error handling for the get_item route. If an item is not found, we return a 404 status code along with an error message.

You can enhance error handling further by checking for potential issues in the create_item route. For example, you might want to validate the incoming data before creating a new item:

python
Copy code
```python
@app.route('/items', methods=['POST'])
def create_item():
new_item = request.get_json()
if 'name' not in new_item:
return jsonify({"error": "Name is required"}), 400
new_item['id'] = len(items) + 1
items.append(new_item)
return jsonify(new_item), 201
```

In this code, we check if the name field is present in the incoming JSON. If not, we return a 400 Bad Request status with an appropriate error message.

Conclusion

Building your first Flask API is a rewarding experience that sets the foundation for developing more complex applications. In this chapter, you learned how to set up a basic Flask application, define routes for handling various HTTP requests, and return JSON responses. You also explored essential concepts such as error handling and data validation.

With this knowledge, you are now equipped to expand your API further and explore additional features and functionalities. In the next chapters, we will delve deeper into Flask's capabilities, including data persistence, authentication, and more, enabling you to create robust and scalable RESTful APIs.

Chapter 5

Data Persistence with Flask: Integrating SQLAlchemy

In this chapter, we will explore how to integrate SQLAlchemy into your Flask application to manage data persistence. SQLAlchemy is a powerful Object Relational Mapper (ORM) that allows developers to interact with databases using Python objects rather than raw SQL queries. This abstraction simplifies database operations and enhances code readability and maintainability.

We will cover setting up SQLAlchemy, creating a database model, performing CRUD operations, and handling migrations. By the end of this chapter, you will be able to persist data in a database and manage it effectively within your Flask application.

Understanding SQLAlchemy

SQLAlchemy provides a set of high-level APIs for interacting with databases. It consists of two main components: the SQL Expression Language and the ORM. The SQL Expression Language allows you to construct SQL queries in a Pythonic way, while the ORM lets you map Python classes to database tables.

This chapter focuses on using the ORM to handle data persistence, allowing you to define models that represent your database tables and manipulate data using Python objects.

Setting Up SQLAlchemy in Your Flask Application

To begin using SQLAlchemy, you need to install the necessary packages. In your active virtual environment, run the following command:

bash
Copy code
```
pip install Flask-SQLAlchemy
```

Once installed, you can integrate SQLAlchemy into your Flask application. Open your app.py file and modify it as follows:

Configuring the Database

Import SQLAlchemy: Import the SQLAlchemy class from the flask_sqlalchemy module.
Set Up Configuration: Configure your Flask app to connect to a database. You can use SQLite for simplicity,

but SQLAlchemy supports various database backends, including PostgreSQL, MySQL, and others.

Here's how you can set up your application to use SQLAlchemy with an SQLite database:

python
Copy code
```
from flask import Flask, jsonify, request
from flask_sqlalchemy import SQLAlchemy

app = Flask(__name__)
app.config['SQLALCHEMY_DATABASE_URI']        =
'sqlite:///items.db'
app.config['SQLALCHEMY_TRACK_MODIFICATIO
NS'] = False

db = SQLAlchemy(app)
```

In this code, we specify the database URI for SQLite (sqlite:///items.db), which creates a file named items.db in the project directory. The SQLALCHEMY_TRACK_MODIFICATIONS setting is disabled to suppress warnings.

Creating a Database Model

With SQLAlchemy configured, the next step is to define a database model. A model represents a table in your database and provides a way to interact with the data in that table.

Let's create a simple model for our items:

python
Copy code
```
class Item(db.Model):
id = db.Column(db.Integer, primary_key=True)
name = db.Column(db.String(80), nullable=False)

def __repr__(self):
return f'<Item {self.name}>'
```

In this model:

Item is a class that inherits from db.Model, making it a SQLAlchemy model.
The id column is defined as an integer and serves as the primary key for the table.
The name column is defined as a string with a maximum length of 80 characters and cannot be null.

Creating the Database

Once your model is defined, you need to create the database and the corresponding table. You can do this using the Flask shell or by adding a few lines of code in your app.py.

To create the database and table, add the following code at the end of your app.py file:

```python
Copy code
with app.app_context():
db.create_all()
```

This code creates all the tables defined in your models. You should run your application once to execute this code, which will create the items table in the SQLite database.

Performing CRUD Operations

Now that you have a database set up, let's implement CRUD (Create, Read, Update, Delete) operations for managing items. We will modify our routes to interact with the Item model instead of using a simple list.

Creating an Item (POST)

Update the create_item route to save new items to the database:

python
Copy code

```python
@app.route('/items', methods=['POST'])
def create_item():
new_item = request.get_json()
if 'name' not in new_item:
return jsonify({"error": "Name is required"}), 400

item = Item(name=new_item['name'])
db.session.add(item)
db.session.commit()
return jsonify({"id": item.id, "name": item.name}), 201
```

In this code, we create a new Item instance, add it to the session, and commit the session to save the item in the database.

Retrieving All Items (GET)

Next, update the get_items route to retrieve items from the database:

python
Copy code

```python
@app.route('/items', methods=['GET'])
def get_items():
items = Item.query.all()
```

return jsonify([{"id": item.id, "name": item.name} for item in items])

This code uses Item.query.all() to fetch all items from the database and returns them in JSON format.

Retrieving a Specific Item (GET)

Update the get_item route to retrieve a specific item from the database:

python
Copy code

```
@app.route('/items/<int:item_id>', methods=['GET'])
def get_item(item_id):
item = Item.query.get(item_id)
if item is not None:
return jsonify({"id": item.id, "name": item.name})
return jsonify({"error": "Item not found"}), 404
```

Here, we use Item.query.get(item_id) to find the item by its ID. If found, we return the item; otherwise, we return a 404 error.

Updating an Item (PUT)

Now, let's implement the update functionality. Add the following route:

48

python
Copy code

```python
@app.route('/items/<int:item_id>', methods=['PUT'])
def update_item(item_id):
    item = Item.query.get(item_id)
    if item is None:
        return jsonify({"error": "Item not found"}), 404

    updated_data = request.get_json()
    if 'name' in updated_data:
        item.name = updated_data['name']
    db.session.commit()
    return jsonify({"id": item.id, "name": item.name})
```

In this route, we first retrieve the item. If it exists, we update its attributes with the data from the request body and commit the session to save the changes.

Deleting an Item (DELETE)

Finally, add the route to delete an item:

python
Copy code

```python
@app.route('/items/<int:item_id>',
methods=['DELETE'])
def delete_item(item_id):
    item = Item.query.get(item_id)
```

```python
if item is None:
    return jsonify({"error": "Item not found"}), 404

db.session.delete(item)
db.session.commit()
return jsonify({"message": "Item deleted successfully"}),
204
```

This route retrieves the item, deletes it from the session, and commits the session to remove it from the database. It returns a 204 status code to indicate successful deletion.

Handling Migrations with Flask-Migrate

As your application grows and the database schema evolves, managing changes to your models becomes essential. Flask-Migrate is a great tool for handling database migrations using Alembic, which is a database migration tool for SQLAlchemy.

Installing Flask-Migrate

To use Flask-Migrate, install it in your virtual environment:

bash
Copy code
```bash
pip install Flask-Migrate
```

Integrating Flask-Migrate

After installing, you need to set it up in your application. Open your app.py and add the following:

python
Copy code
```
from flask_migrate import Migrate

migrate = Migrate(app, db)
```

Creating a Migration Repository

With Flask-Migrate set up, you can create a migration repository. Run the following commands in your terminal:

bash
Copy code
```
flask db init
flask db migrate -m "Initial migration."
flask db upgrade
```

flask db init: Initializes a new migration repository.
flask db migrate -m "Initial migration.": Generates migration scripts based on your model definitions.
flask db upgrade: Applies the migrations to the database.

Making Changes to Your Model

If you decide to make changes to your Item model, for example, adding a description field, simply modify the model:

python
Copy code
```
class Item(db.Model):
id = db.Column(db.Integer, primary_key=True)
name = db.Column(db.String(80), nullable=False)
description = db.Column(db.String(200), nullable=True)
# New field
```

After making the change, you can create and apply a new migration:

bash
Copy code
```
flask db migrate -m "Added description field."
flask db upgrade
```

This will generate and apply a migration to update the database schema.

Testing the CRUD Operations

With all routes and database interactions set up, you can now test your CRUD operations using Postman or Curl:

Create a New Item: Send a POST request to /items with a JSON body to create a new item.

Retrieve All Items: Send a GET request to /items to fetch the list of items.

Retrieve a Specific Item: Send a GET request to /items/<item_id> to fetch a specific item.

Update an Item: Send a PUT request to /items/<item_id> with a JSON body to update an existing item.

Delete an Item: Send a DELETE request to /items/<item_id> to remove an item.

Chapter 6

Building a RESTful API with Django REST Framework

In this chapter, we will delve into building a RESTful API using the Django REST Framework (DRF). Django is a high-level web framework that encourages rapid development and clean, pragmatic design. When combined with DRF, it becomes a powerful tool for creating RESTful APIs with minimal effort.

We will cover the installation and setup of Django and DRF, creating models, views, serializers, and routing. By the end of this chapter, you will be equipped to develop robust APIs using Django.

Introduction to Django REST Framework

Django REST Framework is a powerful toolkit for building Web APIs in Django. It provides a flexible and modular architecture that helps developers create APIs quickly and efficiently. With DRF, you can leverage Django's built-in features, such as authentication and permissions, while also taking advantage of powerful tools for serialization and query handling.

DRF emphasizes simplicity and reusability, enabling you to write less code while achieving more functionality. It supports various features like authentication, serialization, and view sets, making it an excellent choice for building APIs.

Setting Up a Django Project

Before diving into the specifics of DRF, you need to set up a Django project. Here are the steps to get started:

Installing Django and Django REST Framework

First, ensure you have Django and DRF installed in your virtual environment. Run the following commands:

```bash
Copy code
pip install Django
pip install djangorestframework
```

Creating a New Django Project

Next, create a new Django project and an application within that project:

```bash
Copy code
```

```
django-admin startproject myproject
cd myproject
django-admin startapp myapp
```

This creates a new directory called myproject, containing the core project files, and a subdirectory called myapp for your application logic.

Configuring the Project

Open the settings.py file in the myproject directory and add rest_framework and your app (myapp) to the INSTALLED_APPS list:

```python
Copy code
INSTALLED_APPS = [
...
'rest_framework',
'myapp',
]
```

This informs Django that you are using the Django REST Framework and your custom application.

Creating a Database Model

In DRF, you define models similar to how you would in standard Django applications. These models represent the data structure in your database. Let's create a simple model for an item in models.py within myapp:

python
Copy code

```python
from django.db import models

class Item(models.Model):
    name = models.CharField(max_length=80)
    description = models.TextField(blank=True, null=True)

    def __str__(self):
        return self.name
```

In this code, we define an Item model with two fields: name and description. The name field is a character field with a maximum length of 80 characters, while the description field is optional.

Migrating the Model

After defining your model, you need to create the corresponding database table. Run the following commands to create and apply migrations:

bash

Copy code

```
python manage.py makemigrations
python manage.py migrate
```

These commands create migration files and apply them to your database, setting up the Item table.

Creating Serializers

Serializers in DRF are responsible for converting complex data types, such as Django models, into native Python data types that can then be easily rendered into JSON. They also handle validation when creating or updating data.

Defining a Serializer

Create a new file called serializers.py in the myapp directory and define a serializer for the Item model:

python
Copy code

```
from rest_framework import serializers
from .models import Item

class ItemSerializer(serializers.ModelSerializer):
    class Meta:
        model = Item
        fields = ['id', 'name', 'description']
```

In this code, we create an ItemSerializer class that inherits from serializers.ModelSerializer. The Meta class specifies which model to serialize and which fields to include.

Creating Views

Next, we need to create views to handle HTTP requests. DRF provides several types of views, but we will focus on using viewsets, which combine the logic for multiple related views into a single class.

Defining a ViewSet

Open views.py in your myapp directory and define a viewset for the Item model:

```python
Copy code
from rest_framework import viewsets
from .models import Item
from .serializers import ItemSerializer

class ItemViewSet(viewsets.ModelViewSet):
queryset = Item.objects.all()
serializer_class = ItemSerializer
```

In this code, ItemViewSet inherits from viewsets.ModelViewSet, providing CRUD operations without additional code. The queryset attribute specifies the data to be operated on, and the serializer_class indicates which serializer to use.

Setting Up URLs

To make your API accessible, you need to define URL patterns. Create a new file called urls.py in your myapp directory and set up routing for your viewset:

```python
Copy code
from django.urls import path, include
from rest_framework.routers import DefaultRouter
from .views import ItemViewSet

router = DefaultRouter()
router.register(r'items', ItemViewSet)

urlpatterns = [
    path('', include(router.urls)),
]
```

In this code, we create a DefaultRouter, register the ItemViewSet, and include the router's URLs in the app's URL configuration.

Next, include the app's URLs in the project's main urls.py file located in the myproject directory:

python
Copy code
```
from django.contrib import admin
from django.urls import path, include

urlpatterns = [
path('admin/', admin.site.urls),
path('api/', include('myapp.urls')),
]
```

With this setup, your API endpoints will be accessible at /api/items/.

Testing Your API

Now that your API is set up, you can test it using tools like Postman or Curl. Here are the endpoints you can access:

GET /api/items/: Retrieve a list of all items.
POST /api/items/: Create a new item. Send a JSON payload with the name and optional description fields.
GET /api/items/<id>/: Retrieve a specific item by ID.
PUT /api/items/<id>/: Update an existing item by sending a JSON payload.

61

DELETE /api/items/<id>/: Delete a specific item by ID.

Authentication and Permissions

Django REST Framework comes with built-in authentication and permission classes to secure your API. You can easily implement token authentication or session authentication.

Setting Up Token Authentication

To enable token authentication, first, install the djangorestframework-simplejwt **package:**

bash
Copy code
```
pip install djangorestframework-simplejwt
```

Next, update your settings.py file to include authentication classes:

python
Copy code
```
REST_FRAMEWORK = {
'DEFAULT_AUTHENTICATION_CLASSES': (
'rest_framework_simplejwt.authentication.JWTAuthenti
cation',
),
```

```
'DEFAULT_PERMISSION_CLASSES': (
'rest_framework.permissions.IsAuthenticated',
),
}
```

This configuration requires authentication for all API endpoints. You can customize permissions based on your application's needs.

Creating a Token View

To enable users to obtain tokens, add a new endpoint in your urls.py:

python
Copy code
```
from rest_framework_simplejwt.views import TokenObtainPairView

urlpatterns = [
path('api/token/', TokenObtainPairView.as_view(),
name='token_obtain_pair'),
path(", include(router.urls)),
]
```

Now users can request tokens by sending a POST request to /api/token/ with their credentials.

Handling Permissions

DRF allows you to manage permissions easily. You can specify permission classes at the view level or globally in your settings. Here's an example of how to implement custom permissions:

python
Copy code
```python
from rest_framework.permissions import BasePermission

class IsOwner(BasePermission):
def has_object_permission(self, request, view, obj):
return obj.owner == request.user
```

You can then apply this permission to your viewset:

python
Copy code
```python
class ItemViewSet(viewsets.ModelViewSet):
queryset = Item.objects.all()
serializer_class = ItemSerializer
permission_classes = [IsOwner]
```

With this setup, only the owner of an item can modify or delete it.

Conclusion

In this chapter, we explored how to build a RESTful API using Django and Django REST Framework. You learned how to set up a Django project, define models, create serializers, and implement CRUD operations using viewsets. We also covered authentication, permissions, and how to secure your API.

With these foundations, you are well-equipped to build more complex APIs with advanced features such as pagination, filtering, and more. In the following chapters, we will delve into these advanced topics and explore best practices for deploying your Django REST API.

Chapter 7

Advanced Topics in RESTful API Development

In this chapter, we will delve into advanced topics related to RESTful API development using both Flask and Django REST Framework. Understanding these concepts will allow you to create more efficient, secure, and scalable APIs. We will cover pagination, filtering, serialization, authentication, and performance optimization strategies. By mastering these topics, you can elevate your API to meet professional standards and user expectations.

Pagination in APIs

Pagination is a crucial technique for managing large sets of data. It allows clients to retrieve data in manageable chunks rather than overwhelming them with massive datasets. Both Flask and Django REST Framework offer built-in support for pagination.

Implementing Pagination in Django REST Framework

DRF provides several pagination classes that you can use to implement pagination effortlessly. The most common classes are PageNumberPagination, LimitOffsetPagination, and CursorPagination.

PageNumberPagination Example

To use PageNumberPagination, update your settings to include a default pagination class:

```python
Copy code
REST_FRAMEWORK = {
'DEFAULT_PAGINATION_CLASS':
'rest_framework.pagination.PageNumberPagination',
'PAGE_SIZE': 10,
}
```

With this configuration, your API will automatically paginate responses. For example, to fetch the second page of items, a client would request /api/items/?page=2. The response will include only 10 items, along with metadata about the total number of pages.

Implementing Pagination in Flask

In Flask, you can implement pagination manually or use extensions like Flask-SQLAlchemy for more convenient querying. Here's a simple example of manual pagination:

python
Copy code
```
@app.route('/items', methods=['GET'])
def get_items():
page = request.args.get('page', 1, type=int)
per_page = request.args.get('per_page', 10, type=int)
items    =    Item.query.paginate(page,    per_page,
error_out=False)
return jsonify({
'items': [{"id": item.id, "name": item.name} for item in
items.items],
'total': items.total,
'pages': items.pages,
'current_page': items.page,
})
```

In this code, we retrieve the page and per_page parameters from the query string. The paginate method returns an object containing the current page of items and pagination metadata.

Filtering API Responses

Filtering allows clients to refine their search results based on specific criteria. This feature enhances user experience by making data retrieval more efficient.

Filtering in Django REST Framework

DRF provides robust support for filtering through Django's ORM capabilities. You can use the FilterSet class from django_filters to create filters easily.

Setting Up Filtering

First, install django-filter:

bash
Copy code
```
pip install django-filter
```

Next, update your settings to include the filter backend:

python
Copy code
```
REST_FRAMEWORK = {
'DEFAULT_FILTER_BACKENDS': (
'django_filters.rest_framework.DjangoFilterBackend',
),
}
```

Then, create a filter for your Item model:

python
Copy code
```python
import django_filters

class ItemFilter(django_filters.FilterSet):
class Meta:
model = Item
fields = ['name', 'description']
```

Finally, add the filter to your viewset:

python
Copy code
```python
from rest_framework import filters

class ItemViewSet(viewsets.ModelViewSet):
queryset = Item.objects.all()
serializer_class = ItemSerializer
filterset_class = ItemFilter
filter_backends = (filters.DjangoFilterBackend,)
```

Clients can now filter items by specifying query parameters, such as /api/items/?name=example.

Filtering in Flask

In Flask, you can implement filtering by applying query parameters directly in your routes. Here's how you can set it up:

python
Copy code
```
@app.route('/items', methods=['GET'])
def get_items():
query = request.args.get('name')
if query:
items                                        =
Item.query.filter(Item.name.contains(query)).all()
else:
items = Item.query.all()

return jsonify([{"id": item.id, "name": item.name} for
item in items])
```

In this example, the API filters items based on the name query parameter.

Serialization and Deserialization

Serialization is the process of converting complex data types, like Django models or SQLAlchemy objects, into JSON or XML. Deserialization is the reverse process— converting JSON back into complex data types.

Advanced Serialization in Django REST Framework

DRF serializers can handle complex nested objects, relationships, and validation. For instance, if your Item model has a foreign key relationship to another model, you can include related data in your serializer.

Defining a Nested Serializer

Suppose you have a Category model:

```python
Copy code
class Category(models.Model):
    name = models.CharField(max_length=50)
```

You can create a nested serializer:

```python
Copy code
class CategorySerializer(serializers.ModelSerializer):
    class Meta:
        model = Category
        fields = ['id', 'name']

class ItemSerializer(serializers.ModelSerializer):
    category = CategorySerializer()

    class Meta:
```

```
model = Item
fields = ['id', 'name', 'description', 'category']
```

This setup allows you to include category information when serializing items.

Serialization in Flask

In Flask, you can manually create serialization logic within your models or use libraries like Marshmallow for more complex scenarios. Here's an example of serialization in Flask:

```python
Copy code
class ItemSchema(ma.SQLAlchemyAutoSchema):
class Meta:
model = Item

@app.route('/items', methods=['GET'])
def get_items():
items = Item.query.all()
schema = ItemSchema(many=True)
return schema.jsonify(items)
```

This example utilizes Marshmallow to automate the serialization process.

Authentication and Security

Securing your API is paramount. Implementing proper authentication mechanisms will ensure that only authorized users can access or modify your data.

Implementing Token Authentication in Django REST Framework

DRF provides a built-in mechanism for token authentication. To enable this, ensure you have the rest_framework.authtoken package included in your INSTALLED_APPS.

After installing the necessary packages, you can create a view for token authentication:

```python
Copy code
from rest_framework.authtoken.views import ObtainAuthToken

urlpatterns = [
path('api/token-auth/', ObtainAuthToken.as_view()),
]
```

Clients can send a POST request to /api/token-auth/ with their username and password to receive an authentication token.

Implementing JWT Authentication in Flask

In Flask, you can implement JWT (JSON Web Tokens) for authentication using the Flask-JWT-Extended package. First, install the package:

```bash
Copy code
pip install Flask-JWT-Extended
```

Next, configure it in your Flask application:

```python
Copy code
from flask_jwt_extended import JWTManager

app.config['JWT_SECRET_KEY'] = 'your_jwt_secret_key'
jwt = JWTManager(app)
```

You can create login and token generation routes:

```python
Copy code
```

```
@app.route('/login', methods=['POST'])
def login():
username = request.json.get('username')
password = request.json.get('password')
user = User.query.filter_by(username=username).first()

if user and user.verify_password(password):
access_token = create_access_token(identity=user.id)
return jsonify(access_token=access_token), 200
return jsonify({"msg": "Bad username or password"}),
401
```

This example illustrates how to generate a token upon successful login.

Performance Optimization Strategies

Optimizing API performance is essential for a responsive user experience. Here are some strategies for both Flask and Django:

Caching Responses

Implementing caching can significantly reduce load times and server strain. Use libraries like django-cacheops for Django or Flask-Caching for Flask to cache query results.

Using Select Related and Prefetch Related

In Django, you can use select_related and prefetch_related to optimize database queries when working with related models. This minimizes the number of database hits:

```python
Copy code
queryset = Item.objects.select_related('category').all()
```

Optimizing Queries in Flask

In Flask, ensure you are using efficient queries. For example, use with_entities to select only the required fields instead of fetching entire rows.

Rate Limiting

Implementing rate limiting can protect your API from abuse. You can use packages like django-ratelimit for Django or Flask-Limiter for Flask to limit the number of requests a client can make in a given time frame.

Conclusion

In this chapter, we explored advanced topics in RESTful API development, focusing on pagination, filtering, serialization, authentication, and performance optimization. These concepts are essential for building scalable and efficient APIs. As you continue to develop your API, consider how you can implement these strategies to enhance functionality and user experience. In the next chapter, we will look into best practices for deploying your APIs securely and efficiently.

Chapter 8

Best Practices for RESTful API Development

In this chapter, we will explore the best practices for developing RESTful APIs, focusing on both Flask and Django REST Framework. Following these best practices will ensure that your APIs are not only efficient and secure but also user-friendly and maintainable. We'll cover aspects such as API design principles, versioning, error handling, documentation, and security measures.

API Design Principles

A well-designed API is crucial for ensuring usability and maintainability. Following certain design principles can lead to a more intuitive and consistent API.

Resource-Based Architecture

RESTful APIs should be designed around resources rather than actions. Each resource should be represented by a unique URL. For example, instead of creating endpoints like /createUser or /getUser, your API should expose a resource-based endpoint structure:

POST /api/users/ for creating a user
GET /api/users/{id}/ for retrieving a user
PUT /api/users/{id}/ for updating a user
DELETE /api/users/{id}/ for deleting a user

By adopting this resource-based approach, you can make your API easier to understand and use.

Use of HTTP Methods

HTTP methods play a crucial role in defining the action to be performed on resources. Use the appropriate HTTP methods to make your API more intuitive:

GET: Retrieve data without causing side effects.
POST: Create a new resource.
PUT: Update an existing resource.
PATCH: Partially update a resource.
DELETE: Remove a resource.

Following this convention not only adheres to REST principles but also aligns with the expectations of developers consuming your API.

Consistent Naming Conventions

Use clear and consistent naming conventions for your endpoints and resource names. Resource names should be plural, and URIs should be lowercased. For example, instead of using UserProfile, use userprofiles. This consistency aids in readability and understanding.

Statelessness

One of the key principles of REST is that APIs should be stateless. Each request from a client should contain all the information necessary to understand and process that request. Avoid maintaining any session state on the server side. This approach simplifies scalability and reliability.

Versioning Your API

As your API evolves, it's important to version it to maintain compatibility with existing clients. Here are common strategies for API versioning:

URI Versioning

One straightforward method is to include the version in the URL. For example:

/api/v1/users/
/api/v2/users/

This method is simple and allows clients to specify which version they want to use.

Header Versioning

Another method involves versioning through custom headers. Clients can specify the API version in the request header:

bash
Copy code
Accept: application/vnd.yourapi.v1+json

While this method keeps the URLs clean, it may be less intuitive for users.

Query Parameter Versioning

You can also use query parameters to indicate the API version:

/api/users?version=1

This method is easy to implement but can clutter your query strings.

Choose the versioning strategy that aligns with your API design and user expectations. Make sure to document your versioning approach clearly for consumers.

Error Handling and Response Codes

Proper error handling is vital for a good developer experience. APIs should return meaningful error messages and appropriate HTTP status codes.

Standard HTTP Status Codes

Use standard HTTP status codes to indicate the result of a request:

200 OK: Successful GET, PUT, or DELETE request.
201 Created: Successful POST request.
204 No Content: Successful DELETE request with no content in the response.
400 Bad Request: Client-side error due to malformed request syntax.
401 Unauthorized: Authentication required or failed.
403 Forbidden: Server understood the request but refuses to authorize it.
404 Not Found: Requested resource could not be found.
500 Internal Server Error: Server encountered an unexpected condition.

Returning Error Messages

Along with HTTP status codes, return meaningful error messages in the response body. This can include an error code, a description, and possibly a suggested fix:

json

Copy code

```
{
"error": {
"code": "USER_NOT_FOUND",
"message": "The user with ID 123 does not exist."
}
}
```

Providing informative error messages will help developers troubleshoot issues more effectively.

Documentation

Comprehensive documentation is crucial for any API, as it enables developers to understand how to use your API effectively. A well-documented API is often more successful in adoption and usage.

Using OpenAPI Specification

The OpenAPI Specification (formerly known as Swagger) is a powerful tool for documenting RESTful APIs. It allows you to define your API structure, endpoints, request and response formats, and authentication methods in a machine-readable format.

Tools like Swagger UI can generate interactive documentation that allows users to test your API directly from the documentation page.

Keep Documentation Updated

Ensure that your API documentation is always up to date. As you make changes to your API, update the documentation accordingly. Outdated documentation can lead to confusion and errors among developers.

Provide Examples

Include examples in your documentation for different use cases, such as authentication, error responses, and data formats. This can help developers quickly understand how to interact with your API.

Security Best Practices

Security is a top priority when developing APIs. Implementing the following best practices will help protect your API from various threats.

Use HTTPS

Always serve your API over HTTPS to encrypt the data transmitted between the client and server. This prevents man-in-the-middle attacks and protects sensitive information, such as authentication tokens and personal data.

Authentication and Authorization

Implement robust authentication mechanisms, such as OAuth 2.0 or JWT, to secure your API endpoints. Ensure that only authenticated users can access protected resources.

Rate Limiting

Implement rate limiting to protect your API from abuse and denial-of-service (DoS) attacks. You can use libraries like django-ratelimit for Django or Flask-Limiter for Flask to set request limits.

Input Validation

Always validate input data to prevent injection attacks, such as SQL injection or cross-site scripting (XSS). Ensure that data types, lengths, and formats conform to expected patterns.

Sanitize Output

Sanitize any output sent to clients to prevent information leakage and ensure that sensitive data is not exposed inadvertently.

Log and Monitor API Usage

Implement logging and monitoring for your API to track usage patterns and detect unusual activities. Tools like ELK Stack or third-party services can help you maintain logs and analyze them for security breaches or performance issues.

Testing Your API

Testing is an essential part of the development process, especially for APIs. Automated tests ensure that your API behaves as expected and helps catch regressions.

Unit Testing

Create unit tests for your API endpoints using frameworks like pytest for Flask or Django's built-in testing framework. Ensure that you cover various scenarios, including both successful and error responses.

Integration Testing

Perform integration tests to check how different parts of your API work together. This can involve testing the interaction between your API and the database, as well as other external services.

Load Testing

Conduct load testing to evaluate how your API performs under heavy traffic. Tools like Apache JMeter or Locust can help simulate multiple users making requests to your API simultaneously.

Conclusion

In this chapter, we covered best practices for RESTful API development, focusing on design principles, versioning, error handling, documentation, security, and testing. Adhering to these best practices will lead to a more robust, user-friendly, and maintainable API. As you continue to develop your API, keep these principles in mind to create a high-quality product that meets user needs and expectations. In the next chapter, we will explore deployment strategies for your APIs, focusing on scalability and reliability.

Chapter 9

Deployment Strategies for RESTful APIs

In this chapter, we will delve into the deployment strategies for RESTful APIs built with Flask and Django REST Framework. A well-planned deployment process is crucial for ensuring that your API is accessible, scalable, and secure. We will cover various deployment environments, best practices for server configuration, containerization, and continuous integration and deployment (CI/CD) practices. By the end of this chapter, you will have a comprehensive understanding of how to effectively deploy and maintain your API in a production environment.

Deployment Environments

When deploying your API, you have several options for hosting environments, each with its own benefits and trade-offs.

Cloud Services

Cloud platforms like AWS, Google Cloud, and Azure provide scalable infrastructure for deploying APIs. They offer various services, such as virtual machines (VMs), serverless functions, and container orchestration, making it easier to manage and scale your applications.

Using AWS Elastic Beanstalk

AWS Elastic Beanstalk is a popular choice for deploying Flask and Django applications. It simplifies the deployment process by managing the underlying infrastructure. You simply upload your application, and Elastic Beanstalk handles the rest, including provisioning, load balancing, and scaling.

To deploy your application with Elastic Beanstalk, follow these steps:

Install   the   Elastic   Beanstalk   CLI:
bash
Copy   code

```
pip install awsebcli
```

Initialize   your   Elastic   Beanstalk   application:
bash
Copy   code

```
eb init -p python-3.8 your-app-name
```

Create an environment and deploy:
bash
Copy   code
```
eb create your-env-name
eb deploy
```

Containerization with Docker

Containerization is an effective way to package your application and its dependencies. Docker allows you to create lightweight containers that can run consistently across different environments.

Creating a Dockerfile

To deploy your API using Docker, create a Dockerfile in the root of your project:

dockerfile
Copy code
```
# Use an official Python runtime as a parent image
FROM python:3.8-slim

# Set the working directory in the container
WORKDIR /app
```

91

```
# Copy the current directory contents into the container at
/app
COPY . /app

# Install any needed packages specified in
requirements.txt
RUN pip install --no-cache-dir -r requirements.txt

# Make port 80 available to the world outside this
container
EXPOSE 80

# Define environment variable
ENV NAME World

# Run the application
CMD ["gunicorn", "-b", "0.0.0.0:80", "yourapp:app"]
```

With this Dockerfile, you can build and run your application in a Docker container.

Using Kubernetes

Kubernetes is a powerful orchestration tool for managing containerized applications. If your API requires high availability and scalability, Kubernetes can help manage multiple instances of your application.

Deploying to Kubernetes

Create a Deployment YAML file:
yaml
Copy   code

```
apiVersion: apps/v1
kind: Deployment
metadata:
name: your-api
spec:
replicas: 3
selector:
matchLabels:
app: your-api
template:
metadata:
labels:
app: your-api
spec:
containers:
name: your-api
image: your-docker-image
ports:
containerPort: 80
```

Apply   the   deployment:
bash

```
kubectl apply -f deployment.yaml
```

By using Kubernetes, you can manage the scaling, load balancing, and rolling updates of your application seamlessly.

Server Configuration

When deploying your API, proper server configuration is essential for performance, security, and reliability.

Choosing a Web Server

Select a suitable web server for serving your API. Common choices include:

Gunicorn: A Python WSGI HTTP server that is lightweight and simple to use. It works well with Flask and Django.
Nginx: A high-performance web server that can act as a reverse proxy, load balancer, and HTTP cache. It is often used in conjunction with Gunicorn.

Configuring Nginx with Gunicorn

To set up Nginx as a reverse proxy for your Gunicorn server, follow these steps:

Install **Nginx**:

bash

Copy code

```bash
sudo apt update
sudo apt install nginx
```

Configure Nginx: Create a configuration file in /etc/nginx/sites-available/yourapp:

nginx

Copy code

```nginx
server {
listen 80;
server_name yourdomain.com;

location / {
proxy_pass http://127.0.0.1:8000;  # Gunicorn server
proxy_set_header Host $host;
proxy_set_header X-Real-IP $remote_addr;
proxy_set_header X-Forwarded-For $proxy_add_x_forwarded_for;
proxy_set_header X-Forwarded-Proto $scheme;
}
}
```

Enable the configuration:

bash

Copy code

```
sudo ln -s /etc/nginx/sites-available/yourapp
/etc/nginx/sites-enabled
sudo systemctl restart nginx
```

Setting Up SSL

To secure your API, set up SSL using Let's Encrypt:

Install Certbot:

bash

Copy code

```
sudo apt install certbot python3-certbot-nginx
```

Obtain an SSL certificate:

bash

Copy code

```
sudo certbot --nginx -d yourdomain.com
```

Certbot will automatically configure Nginx to redirect HTTP traffic to HTTPS, ensuring your API is served securely.

Continuous Integration and Deployment (CI/CD)

Implementing CI/CD practices can streamline your deployment process and enhance code quality.

Setting Up CI/CD with GitHub Actions

GitHub Actions is a powerful CI/CD tool that allows you to automate your workflow. You can create a .github/workflows/deploy.yml file in your repository:

```yaml
Copy code
name: Deploy to Production

on:
push:
branches:
main

jobs:
deploy:
runs-on: ubuntu-latest
steps:
name: Checkout code
uses: actions/checkout@v2

name: Set up Python
uses: actions/setup-python@v2
```

```
with:
python-version: '3.8'

name: Install dependencies
run: |
pip install -r requirements.txt

name: Build Docker image
run: |
docker build -t your-image-name .

name: Push Docker image
run: |
echo "${{ secrets.DOCKER_PASSWORD }}" | docker
login -u "${{ secrets.DOCKER_USERNAME }}" --
password-stdin
docker push your-image-name

name: Deploy to Server
run: |
ssh user@your-server 'docker pull your-image-name &&
docker run -d -p 80:80 your-image-name'
```

This workflow automates the deployment process every time you push changes to the main branch.

Using Travis CI or CircleCI

Alternatively, you can use other CI/CD tools like Travis CI or CircleCI. These platforms allow you to define build and deployment pipelines, ensuring that your code is tested and deployed automatically.

Monitoring and Logging

Once your API is deployed, monitoring and logging are essential for maintaining performance and reliability.

Monitoring Tools

Use monitoring tools like Prometheus, Grafana, or New Relic to keep track of your API's performance. These tools provide insights into metrics such as response time, error rates, and traffic patterns.

Logging Best Practices

Implement logging to capture important events and errors in your API. Use libraries like loguru for Flask or Django's built-in logging module. Ensure that logs are written to a central location, making it easier to access and analyze them.

Here's an example of setting up logging in Django:

python
Copy code

```
import logging

logger = logging.getLogger(__name__)

def my_view(request):
logger.info('This is an info message.')
return HttpResponse('Hello, world!')
```

For Flask, you can configure logging in your application:

python
Copy code
```
import logging

logging.basicConfig(level=logging.INFO)

@app.route('/')
def hello():
app.logger.info('Hello endpoint was hit')
return 'Hello, World!'
```

Scaling Your API

As your API usage grows, you may need to consider scaling strategies.

Horizontal Scaling

Horizontal scaling involves adding more instances of your application. This can be achieved using load balancers to distribute traffic among multiple servers.

Vertical Scaling

Vertical scaling involves upgrading your existing server resources, such as CPU, RAM, and storage. While this approach is simpler, it has limitations compared to horizontal scaling.

Using a Load Balancer

A load balancer can distribute incoming traffic among multiple instances of your API, improving responsiveness and availability. Tools like AWS Elastic Load Balancing or Nginx can help manage this distribution.

Conclusion

In this chapter, we explored deployment strategies for RESTful APIs, focusing on deployment environments, server configuration, CI/CD practices, monitoring, logging, and scaling. Understanding these strategies will enable you to deploy and maintain your API effectively in a production environment. In the next chapter, we will cover API versioning in depth, discussing strategies for managing changes and maintaining backward compatibility.

Chapter 10

API Versioning Strategies

In this chapter, we will delve into API versioning, a crucial aspect of RESTful API development that allows you to manage changes and maintain backward compatibility. As your API evolves, it is essential to provide a way for clients to transition to new versions without breaking their existing applications. We will explore different versioning strategies, their advantages and disadvantages, and best practices for implementing versioning in your Flask and Django REST Framework APIs.

Why Version Your API?

APIs are living entities that evolve over time due to feature enhancements, bug fixes, and performance improvements. Versioning is essential for several reasons:

Backward Compatibility

When you introduce changes to your API, you risk breaking existing clients. Versioning allows you to release new features while ensuring that older clients continue to function without disruption.

Client Flexibility

With versioning, clients can choose when to adopt the latest API changes. This flexibility is crucial for organizations with extensive integrations, as they may not be able to upgrade immediately.

Clear Documentation

Versioning provides a structured way to document changes. By specifying version numbers, developers can quickly understand the differences between various iterations of the API.

Common Versioning Strategies

There are several strategies for versioning your API, each with its own advantages and trade-offs. Let's explore the most common approaches.

URI Versioning

URI versioning involves including the version number directly in the URL. This method is one of the simplest and most widely adopted approaches.

Advantages

Simplicity: Easy to implement and understand.

Clear visibility: Users can quickly identify the API version they are working with.

Example

A typical URI versioning scheme might look like this:

```
GET /api/v1/users/
GET /api/v2/users/
```

Header Versioning

Header versioning involves specifying the API version in the request headers rather than the URL. Clients send a custom header indicating the desired version.

Advantages

Cleaner URLs: Keeps the API endpoints clean and focused on resources.
Flexible versioning: Allows for more complex versioning schemes beyond simple numeric versions.

Example

A request with header versioning might look like this:

```bash
Copy code
GET /api/users/
```

Headers:
Accept: application/vnd.yourapi.v1+json

Query Parameter Versioning

In this approach, the version number is specified as a query parameter in the request URL.

Advantages

Easy to implement: Simple to set up and modify.
Useful for specific endpoints: Allows different endpoints to be versioned independently.

Example

A query parameter versioning scheme might look like this:

```bash
Copy code
GET /api/users?version=1
```

Media Type Versioning

This strategy involves using the media type in the Content-Type or Accept headers to specify the version.

Advantages

Rich semantic meaning: Clearly communicates the intended response format along with versioning.
Flexible and extensible: Can accommodate multiple versions and formats easily.

Example

A media type versioning request might look like:

```bash
Copy code
GET /api/users/
Headers:
Accept: application/vnd.yourapi.v1+json
```

Best Practices for API Versioning

To effectively implement versioning in your API, consider the following best practices:

Choose a Versioning Strategy Early

Decide on a versioning strategy early in your API development process. Consistency is key, and making changes to your versioning approach later can lead to confusion and technical debt.

Document Changes Clearly

Maintain clear documentation for each version of your API. Include information about new features, deprecated endpoints, and breaking changes. Tools like Swagger or OpenAPI can help automate and organize this documentation.

Support Multiple Versions

When introducing a new version, ensure that the previous versions remain operational for a reasonable period. This practice allows clients time to transition to the new version without disruption.

Deprecation Policy

Implement a clear deprecation policy that informs clients when an API version will be sunset. Provide adequate notice, and offer guidance on migrating to the new version.

Version Numbering Scheme

Adopt a clear version numbering scheme. Semantic versioning (MAJOR.MINOR.PATCH) is a widely accepted standard that helps convey the significance of changes. For example, incrementing the MAJOR version for breaking changes and MINOR for backward-compatible additions.

Implementing Versioning in Django REST Framework

Let's explore how to implement API versioning in Django REST Framework.

URI Versioning Example

To implement URI versioning, simply update your URLs to include the version:

```python
Copy code
from django.urls import path
from .views import UserView

urlpatterns = [
    path('api/v1/users/', UserView.as_view(), name='user-list-v1'),
    path('api/v2/users/', UserView.as_view(), name='user-list-v2'),
]
```

Header Versioning Example

For header versioning, you can create a custom middleware to check for the version in the request headers:

python
Copy code
```
class APIVersionMiddleware:
def __init__(self, get_response):
self.get_response = get_response

def __call__(self, request):
version = request.headers.get('Accept', '')
request.version = version.split('+')[1] if '+json' in version else '1'
response = self.get_response(request)
return response
```

Query Parameter Versioning Example

For query parameter versioning, modify your views to check for a version parameter:

python
Copy code
```
from rest_framework.views import APIView
from rest_framework.response import Response

class UserView(APIView):
```

```python
def get(self, request):
    version = request.query_params.get('version', '1')
    # Logic based on version
    return Response({"message": "Hello, World!"})
```

Implementing Versioning in Flask

Now let's look at how to implement API versioning in Flask.

URI Versioning Example

To implement URI versioning in Flask, modify your route definitions:

python
Copy code
```python
from flask import Flask

app = Flask(__name__)

@app.route('/api/v1/users/')
def get_users_v1():
    return {"users": []}

@app.route('/api/v2/users/')
def get_users_v2():
    return {"users": []}
```

Header Versioning Example

For header versioning, you can check the headers in your route handlers:

python
Copy code
```python
from flask import request, jsonify

@app.route('/api/users/', methods=['GET'])
def get_users():
version = request.headers.get('Accept', '')
if 'v1' in version:
return jsonify({"users": []})  # V1 response
elif 'v2' in version:
return jsonify({"users": []})  # V2 response
```

Query Parameter Versioning Example

For query parameter versioning, read the parameters in your route:

python
Copy code
```python
@app.route('/api/users/', methods=['GET'])
def get_users():
```

```
version = request.args.get('version', '1')
if version == '1':
return jsonify({"users": []})  # V1 response
elif version == '2':
return jsonify({"users": []})  # V2 response
```

Conclusion

In this chapter, we explored the importance of API versioning and various strategies for implementing it effectively in your RESTful APIs. We discussed common versioning strategies, best practices, and practical examples for both Django REST Framework and Flask. By adhering to these guidelines, you can ensure a smooth transition for clients when making changes to your API. In the next chapter, we will focus on testing strategies for RESTful APIs, emphasizing the importance of automated testing in maintaining code quality.

Chapter 11

Data Persistence with Django

Setting Up Models in Django

Django's powerful Object-Relational Mapping (ORM) system allows developers to define database schemas directly in Python code through models. Each model is represented as a class, and each class attribute corresponds to a database field. Setting up models begins with understanding the fundamental components of a Django application, particularly how models interact with the database.

When creating a model, the first step is to import the models module from django.db. You can define a model by subclassing models.Model. Each attribute of the model class represents a database column, and the type of the attribute determines the type of the column. For instance, models.CharField is used for character fields, while models.IntegerField is designated for integer values. Defining the fields is not just about declaring their types; it also involves providing various options such as max_length, default, blank, and null.

Consider a simple example of a Book model. In this case, you might define fields such as title, author, and published_date. Each of these fields will need specific parameters. For instance, the title might be a CharField with a maximum length of 200 characters, while the published_date would be a DateField. Django also supports more complex field types such as ForeignKey, ManyToManyField, and OneToOneField, which help establish relationships between models. This is particularly useful for normalizing data and maintaining referential integrity.

Once the model class is defined, you can add metadata through the Meta class. This includes options like verbose_name, which provides a human-readable name for the model, and ordering, which specifies the default ordering of records returned from the database. The Meta class is a powerful feature that allows for fine-tuning the behavior of your model.

After setting up the model, it's crucial to ensure that the model is recognized by Django's migration system. This involves registering the model in an app's models.py file and then creating a migration. Migrations are a way of propagating changes made to the model into the database schema. Running the makemigrations command generates a migration file that contains the operations to create the new model in the database. Following this, the migrate command applies these changes, creating the corresponding database tables.

The process of creating models in Django is designed to be intuitive, allowing developers to focus on building features rather than dealing with database intricacies. This encapsulation of database interactions simplifies the development process, enabling rapid prototyping and iteration.

Performing Migrations and Creating Database Tables

Migrations are an integral part of the Django development process, providing a way to manage changes to your models over time. Once you've defined your models, the next step involves performing migrations to create the actual database tables. This process starts with generating migration files, which are Python scripts that contain the changes made to the models.

The makemigrations command scans the models for any changes and generates migration files accordingly. Each migration file is timestamped and contains a set of operations that describe what changes need to be applied to the database. For example, if you add a new field to an existing model, the migration file will include an operation to add a column in the corresponding database table. Django handles this process automatically, which reduces the likelihood of human error.

Once migration files are generated, the next step is to apply these migrations to the database using the migrate command. This command looks at the migration files and executes the operations in the correct order. If the migration is successful, Django updates its internal records to reflect the applied migrations, ensuring that subsequent migrations can be applied correctly.

One of the key benefits of using migrations in Django is the ability to roll back changes. If you realize that a migration has caused issues, you can use the migrate command with a specific migration name to revert to a previous state. This rollback feature is particularly valuable during the development phase when models and database structures are still evolving. It allows developers to experiment with changes without the fear of permanently losing data or structural integrity.

Additionally, managing migrations in a team environment is facilitated by the version control of migration files. Each developer can generate migrations locally, and then these files can be version-controlled alongside the application code. When changes are pushed to a shared repository, the migration files ensure that everyone on the team can apply the same database structure, preventing conflicts and inconsistencies.

In more advanced scenarios, developers may need to handle migrations manually. This can occur when complex changes are necessary, such as splitting a model into multiple models or changing field types that require data transformations. Django provides tools to create custom migrations, allowing for detailed control over the migration process. However, it's essential to approach manual migrations with caution to avoid introducing errors.

Overall, migrations are a powerful feature in Django that simplifies database management, providing a clear and structured approach to evolving your database schema alongside your application code.

CRUD Operations with Django REST Framework

Django REST Framework (DRF) is a powerful toolkit for building Web APIs in Django. It extends the capabilities of Django, providing a seamless way to implement CRUD (Create, Read, Update, Delete) operations for your models. The framework emphasizes the use of serializers, views, and routers to facilitate API development.

To start implementing CRUD operations, you first need to create a serializer for your model. A serializer in DRF is responsible for converting complex data types such as querysets and model instances into native Python data types that can then be easily rendered into JSON or XML. It also handles the reverse process, validating incoming data and converting it back into model instances.

For example, if you have a Book model, you would create a BookSerializer. This serializer will define the fields that should be included in the API response and also specify validation rules for incoming data. You can customize the serializer by overriding methods like create and update to implement any special handling that your application requires.

Once you have your serializer set up, the next step is to implement views. DRF provides a variety of view classes that can be used to handle HTTP requests. For basic CRUD operations, you might use APIView or GenericAPIView, which provide methods like get, post, put, and delete. These methods correspond to the various CRUD operations, allowing you to define how each HTTP method interacts with your data.

For instance, in the get method, you would retrieve records from the database and return them as a serialized response. In the post method, you would validate incoming data and create a new record in the database. The put method would be used to update an existing record, while delete would remove a record from the database. By organizing your logic within these methods, you maintain a clear separation of concerns, making your codebase easier to manage.

To streamline the routing process, DRF provides a router class that automatically generates URL patterns for your views. This means you can define your API endpoints without manually specifying URL patterns. The router will handle CRUD operations based on the HTTP methods, making it easier to set up a RESTful API.

When implementing CRUD operations, it's essential to consider error handling and validation. DRF provides built-in mechanisms to handle common validation errors, returning appropriate HTTP status codes when something goes wrong. For instance, if a required field is missing in the request data, DRF will automatically respond with a 400 Bad Request status, along with a message detailing the validation error. This level of detail helps clients of your API understand what went wrong and how to correct it.

In addition to basic CRUD operations, DRF also supports more advanced features such as filtering, pagination, and authentication. These features can enhance the usability of your API, allowing clients to interact with your data in a more meaningful way. For instance, you can easily add pagination to limit the number of records returned in a single response, making your API more efficient, especially when dealing with large datasets.

Overall, the Django REST Framework provides a robust and flexible way to implement CRUD operations, allowing you to build powerful APIs that can be easily consumed by clients.

Integrating with Different Database Backends

Django's ORM supports a variety of database backends, which gives developers the flexibility to choose the best database solution for their application. By default, Django comes with built-in support for SQLite, PostgreSQL, MySQL, and Oracle, among others. Each of these databases has its strengths and weaknesses, and understanding how to integrate them with Django is crucial for optimizing your application.

To integrate a different database backend, the first step is to install the appropriate database adapter. For example, if you decide to use PostgreSQL, you need to install the psycopg2 library. For MySQL, the mysqlclient library is commonly used. Once the adapter is installed, you can configure your database settings in the Django project's settings.py file.

The configuration typically involves specifying the ENGINE, NAME, USER, PASSWORD, HOST, and PORT. The ENGINE setting is particularly important, as it tells Django which database backend to use. For PostgreSQL, you would set it to 'django.db.backends.postgresql', while for MySQL, it would be 'django.db.backends.mysql'. The remaining settings configure the connection parameters, allowing Django to authenticate and connect to your database.

Once the database is configured, you can leverage Django's migration system to create the necessary tables in your chosen database. The migration process remains the same, regardless of the backend you choose. After defining your models and running the makemigrations and migrate commands, Django will create the corresponding tables in the specified database.

It's important to note that different databases may have specific features or limitations. For instance, PostgreSQL supports advanced data types such as JSONB, which

Chapter 12

Authentication and authorization in django

Overview of authentication methods in django

Authentication is a critical component of web applications, ensuring that users are who they claim to be before granting access to sensitive resources. Django provides a robust authentication system that supports various methods to authenticate users, making it easier to implement secure authentication flows.

At its core, Django's authentication system includes a user model, authentication backends, and various methods for managing user sessions. The built-in User model provides essential fields such as username, password, email, first name, and last name. This model can be easily extended or replaced to accommodate custom user attributes if your application requires more complex user profiles.

One of the most common methods for authentication in Django is the use of session-based authentication. In this approach, when a user successfully logs in, Django creates a session and stores user information in the session data. This session ID is then sent to the client as a cookie, allowing the user to remain logged in across multiple requests. Django handles session management transparently, providing tools to log users in and out, and to check if a user is authenticated.

Another widely used method is token-based authentication, which is especially popular in RESTful APIs. Instead of maintaining a session, the server issues a token after the user logs in successfully. This token is then sent with each subsequent request, allowing the server to authenticate the user without the need for session management. Django REST Framework (DRF) provides a built-in token authentication system, making it easy to implement this method in your API.

Django also supports third-party authentication methods, such as social authentication via OAuth. This allows users to log in using their social media accounts (like Google, Facebook, or Twitter) rather than creating a new account. Packages such as django-allauth simplify the integration of these third-party providers, offering features like account registration, login, and email verification.

Moreover, Django includes middleware for managing user sessions, which can be customized to fit the security requirements of your application. This middleware ensures that user sessions are secure and helps protect against common security vulnerabilities, such as session fixation and cross-site request forgery (CSRF).

In addition to standard authentication methods, Django provides a way to implement multi-factor authentication (MFA). This adds an additional layer of security by requiring users to provide two or more verification factors to gain access to their accounts. Implementing MFA typically involves integrating an external library or service that can handle the additional verification steps, such as sending a one-time code via SMS or email.

Overall, Django's authentication system is flexible and extensible, allowing developers to implement a wide range of authentication methods tailored to their application's needs.

Implementing token authentication with django rest framework

Token authentication is an essential feature for APIs, particularly those that require stateless authentication. Django REST Framework (DRF) offers built-in support for token authentication, which is a straightforward way to handle user authentication in your API. In this section, we'll explore how to set up and implement token authentication using DRF.

To begin, you'll need to ensure that Django REST Framework and its token authentication package are installed. If you haven't already, you can install DRF using pip. Additionally, you must include rest_framework.authtoken in your INSTALLED_APPS within your Django settings.

Once the package is installed, you can create token instances for your users. This can be accomplished through the Django shell or by using signals. For example, you might want to generate a token automatically when a new user is created. To do this, you can connect to the post_save signal for the User model and create a token for the user each time a new user is added.

The next step is to implement the token authentication mechanism in your API views. DRF provides an ObtainAuthToken view that handles token generation. When a user sends a POST request with their credentials (username and password) to this endpoint, the view authenticates the user. If the credentials are valid, it returns a token that can be used in subsequent requests.

To secure your API endpoints using token authentication, you need to specify the authentication classes in your views or settings. You can do this by adding the TokenAuthentication class to the DEFAULT_AUTHENTICATION_CLASSES in your DRF settings. This ensures that any incoming requests will be authenticated using the token provided in the request headers.

When a client wants to access a protected resource, they need to include the token in the Authorization header of their request. The format for this is Token <your_token>. If the token is valid, DRF will grant access to the view; otherwise, it will return a 401 Unauthorized response.

It's essential to consider token expiration and revocation for enhanced security. By default, tokens do not expire, but you can implement your own expiration logic if needed. This can be achieved by creating a custom authentication class or extending the existing token model to include an expiration field. Additionally, you may want to provide users with a way to revoke their tokens, which can be done by deleting the token from the database.

To improve the security of token authentication, consider using HTTPS to encrypt the communication between the client and server. This prevents attackers from intercepting the token during transmission. Implementing rate limiting and logging failed authentication attempts can also help protect against brute-force attacks.

Overall, token authentication in Django REST Framework is an effective way to handle user authentication in stateless APIs. By following best practices and considering security implications, you can create a robust authentication system for your application.

Managing user permissions and roles

User permissions and roles are crucial for controlling access to various parts of your application. Django provides a powerful permission system that allows developers to specify what actions users can perform on different models. By leveraging this system, you can implement role-based access control, ensuring that users have appropriate permissions based on their roles.

Django's permission system is built on top of its authentication framework, allowing you to define permissions at both the model and object levels. Each model automatically receives three default permissions: add, change, and delete. These permissions can be customized or extended by defining your own in the model's Meta class.

To create custom permissions, you can specify them in the Meta class of your model. For example, if you have a BlogPost model, you might want to add a permission for publishing posts. You would do this by including a permissions attribute in the Meta class, specifying a unique codename and a human-readable name for the permission.

Once you have defined your permissions, you can assign them to users or groups. Django allows for the creation of user groups, making it easier to manage permissions for multiple users. By grouping users with similar access requirements, you can assign permissions to the entire group rather than to each user individually.

To check whether a user has a specific permission, you can use the has_perm method provided by the user model. This method checks the user's permissions against the specified permission codename. For example, you can use request.user.has_perm('app_name.publish_blogpost') to determine if the authenticated user has the permission to publish blog posts.

Django also allows for object-level permissions, which enable you to control access to specific instances of a model. To implement object-level permissions, you may need to use third-party libraries like django-guardian, which provides a straightforward way to handle these permissions. With object-level permissions, you can specify which users can perform actions on individual instances of your models, enhancing the granularity of your access control.

When designing your permission structure, it's essential to follow the principle of least privilege. This means giving users only the permissions they need to perform their job functions, minimizing the risk of unauthorized access or accidental data modification. Regularly reviewing and auditing user permissions can help ensure that your application remains secure and that users have the appropriate access levels.

In addition to permissions, you may also want to implement role-based access control (RBAC) in your application. RBAC allows you to define roles within your system, assigning specific permissions to each role. This approach simplifies permission management and improves security by clearly defining what each role can do.

To implement RBAC, you can create a custom model that represents roles and associate permissions with these roles. When a user is assigned a role, they automatically inherit the permissions associated with that role. This structure makes it easier to manage permissions, especially in larger applications with multiple user types.

In summary, managing user permissions and roles in Django is a powerful way to control access to your application. By leveraging Django's built-in permission system and considering best practices for role-based access control, you can create a secure environment that meets your application's access requirements.

Best practices for securing your django api

Securing your Django API is essential to protect sensitive user data and ensure the integrity of your application. There are several best practices you should follow to enhance the security of your API, minimizing the risk of vulnerabilities and attacks.

First and foremost, always use HTTPS to encrypt data transmitted between the client and server. This prevents attackers from intercepting sensitive information, such as user credentials and authentication tokens. You can obtain an SSL certificate through various providers or use services like Let's Encrypt, which offers free SSL certificates.

Next, implement strong authentication methods. Token authentication is a popular choice for APIs, but ensure that tokens are generated securely and stored safely. Consider adding expiration to tokens and providing mechanisms for users to revoke tokens if necessary. Additionally, always validate incoming data to prevent injection attacks and ensure that the data conforms to expected formats.

Another important aspect of API security is to limit access to your API endpoints. This can be achieved through the use of permissions and role-based access control. Define which users have access to specific endpoints and actions, ensuring that sensitive operations are restricted to authorized personnel only. Regularly audit user permissions to verify that users have appropriate access levels

Chapter 13

Versioning your APIs

Importance of API versioning

API versioning is a crucial aspect of API design and development, ensuring that clients can continue to function correctly as the underlying API evolves. As APIs grow and change over time, versioning becomes necessary to manage changes without disrupting existing clients. This practice allows developers to introduce new features, make improvements, and fix bugs while maintaining backward compatibility for users relying on older versions of the API.

Without versioning, any change to an API—be it a new endpoint, modified response structure, or even a simple parameter change—can break existing clients. This can lead to a poor user experience, as clients that rely on the previous structure may fail to function correctly or produce errors. Therefore, establishing a clear versioning strategy from the outset is essential for maintaining the stability and usability of your API.

There are several common strategies for versioning APIs, each with its pros and cons. One of the most straightforward methods is to include the version number in the URL, such as /api/v1/resource/. This method is explicit, making it clear to users which version of the API they are accessing. It also simplifies routing and version management, as each version can be treated as a separate endpoint within your application.

Another approach is to use request headers to specify the API version. In this case, clients include a custom header (e.g., Accept: application/vnd.yourapi.v1+json) with their requests. This method keeps the URL cleaner and allows for more flexibility in handling versioning. However, it may complicate client implementation, as users need to ensure they set the correct headers.

Media type versioning is a similar approach where the version is included in the Content-Type or Accept headers of the request. This method can be beneficial for APIs that need to support multiple formats (e.g., JSON, XML) while also managing versions. However, like header-based versioning, it may introduce complexity for clients, as they need to handle the correct media type.

Regardless of the versioning strategy you choose, it's important to establish clear documentation to communicate changes and the deprecation of older versions to users. This includes providing a changelog that outlines what changes have been made, what features have been added or removed, and any necessary migration steps for clients upgrading to a new version.

Additionally, consider implementing a deprecation policy for older versions of your API. This policy should specify how long an old version will be supported after a new version is released and outline the process for clients to transition to the latest version. A well-defined deprecation strategy helps ensure that users have sufficient time to adapt their implementations while maintaining the stability of your API.

In summary, API versioning is an essential practice for managing changes and ensuring backward compatibility. By carefully selecting a versioning strategy and communicating effectively with users, you can maintain a stable API while continuing to innovate and improve your services.

Different strategies for versioning APIs (URI, header, media type)

When it comes to versioning APIs, several strategies can be employed, each with distinct advantages and trade-offs. Choosing the right strategy depends on your application's requirements, user base, and the nature of the changes you anticipate making in the future. In this section, we will delve into the most common versioning strategies: URI versioning, header versioning, and media type versioning.

URI versioning is perhaps the most widely adopted method for API versioning. This approach involves including the version number directly in the URL, typically as a path component. For example, an API endpoint might look like this: /api/v1/resource/. The advantages of URI versioning are its clarity and simplicity; users can easily see which version they are interacting with just by looking at the URL. Additionally, routing becomes straightforward, as each version can be treated as a separate resource.

However, URI versioning can lead to URL bloat if not managed carefully. As new versions are released, the number of available endpoints may grow significantly, which can complicate both the client's and server's code. Moreover, URI versioning may not effectively convey changes that are not structural but rather semantic, such as changes in response formats or minor updates that don't warrant a new version.

Header versioning is another approach, where the API version is specified through custom headers in the request. For instance, clients may send requests with a header like Accept: application/vnd.yourapi.v1+json. This method allows for a cleaner URL structure and can support multiple versions and formats simultaneously without cluttering the endpoint paths. However, header versioning may complicate client-side implementation since developers need to ensure that they configure headers correctly for their requests.

Using headers also requires clients to understand the API's expectations, which could lead to confusion if not well-documented. Some users may overlook this requirement, resulting in unexpected errors. Furthermore, debugging issues related to versioning can be more challenging since the version information is not immediately visible in the URL.

Media type versioning is a specific form of header versioning that includes the version in the Content-Type or Accept headers. This approach allows clients to specify the desired response format and version simultaneously. An example might be Accept: application/vnd.yourapi.v1+json. Media type versioning offers the same advantages as header versioning but can be particularly useful for APIs that need to support multiple formats, such as XML or JSON.

However, like header versioning, it can introduce complexity for clients. Users must remember to include the appropriate media type in their requests, and any mistakes could lead to issues with content negotiation. Additionally, not all clients may be equipped to handle media type versioning gracefully, which could result in confusion and increased support requests.

Regardless of the strategy you choose, it's essential to provide comprehensive documentation outlining how versioning works and how clients can access different versions. Clear communication helps users understand the implications of each versioning method and how to adapt their implementations accordingly.

Implementing versioning in flask and django APIs

Implementing API versioning is an essential aspect of maintaining a robust and user-friendly API. In this section, we will explore how to implement versioning in both Flask and Django APIs, focusing on practical examples and best practices.

In Flask, implementing URI versioning is straightforward. You can define routes that include the version number directly in the URL. For example, a basic route might look like this:

```python
Copy code
from flask import Flask, jsonify

app = Flask(__name__)

@app.route('/api/v1/resource', methods=['GET'])
def get_resource_v1():
```

```python
    return jsonify({"message": "This is version 1 of the
resource."})

@app.route('/api/v2/resource', methods=['GET'])
def get_resource_v2():
    return jsonify({"message": "This is version 2 of the
resource."})
```

In this example, two versions of the resource are defined, each with its own route. This approach makes it clear which version of the API the client is accessing and simplifies routing.

For header versioning in Flask, you can access the request headers to check for a version header. Here's how you might implement it:

python
Copy code
```python
from flask import request

@app.route('/api/resource', methods=['GET'])
def get_resource():
    version = request.headers.get('Accept-Version', 'v1')   #
Default to v1 if not specified
    if version == 'v2':
        return jsonify({"message": "This is version 2 of the
resource."})
```

```
else:
return jsonify({"message": "This is version 1 of the
resource."})
```

This method allows clients to specify the version they
want to use, providing a flexible way to handle versioning
without cluttering the URL.

In Django, implementing versioning can be done using a
similar approach with URL patterns. For example, you
might define your URLs in urls.py like this:

python
Copy code
```
from django.urls import path
from .views import ResourceViewV1, ResourceViewV2

urlpatterns = [
path('api/v1/resource/',        ResourceViewV1.as_view(),
name='resource_v1'),
path('api/v2/resource/',        ResourceViewV2.as_view(),
name='resource_v2'),
]
```

Each view can correspond to a specific version, allowing
for clear separation between versions. Additionally,

Django's powerful URL routing capabilities simplify the process of managing multiple versions.

For header-based versioning in Django REST Framework, you can use middleware or customize your view classes to check for versioning headers. Here's an example of how to handle header-based versioning in a DRF view:

python
Copy code
```python
from rest_framework.views import APIView
from rest_framework.response import Response

class ResourceView(APIView):
def get(self, request):
version = request.headers.get('Accept-Version', 'v1')
if version == 'v2':
return Response({"message": "This is version 2 of the resource."})
else:
return Response({"message": "This is version 1 of the resource."})
```

This implementation allows you to serve different responses based on the version specified in the request headers.

When implementing versioning in either Flask or Django, consider using a consistent naming convention for your versions and clearly document how clients should access different versions. Additionally, establish a deprecation policy to guide users through transitioning to newer versions when necessary. This proactive approach to versioning will help maintain a positive experience for users as your API evolves.

Managing backward compatibility

Maintaining backward compatibility is a vital consideration in API design, especially as your API evolves and introduces new features or changes. Backward compatibility ensures that existing clients continue to function correctly, even when new versions of the API are released. This practice is essential for preserving user trust and minimizing disruptions for clients relying on your API.

One of the fundamental strategies for managing backward compatibility is to avoid making breaking changes to the API's core functionality. When introducing new features, consider whether these changes can be implemented in a way that does not affect existing

Chapter 14

Optimizing API performance

Importance of API performance optimization

API performance optimization is essential for ensuring a smooth user experience and maintaining the efficiency of your application. A slow or unresponsive API can frustrate users, leading to increased abandonment rates and diminished user satisfaction. Optimizing API performance not only enhances the user experience but also reduces server load and improves resource utilization, which is particularly important for high-traffic applications.

One key aspect of API performance is response time. Users expect quick responses, and even slight delays can negatively impact their perception of your application. To achieve optimal response times, it's crucial to analyze and identify bottlenecks in your API. This includes examining database queries, network latency, and the overall application architecture.

Another important factor is the number of requests made to the API. Each request adds overhead, so minimizing the number of requests can significantly improve performance. Techniques such as data aggregation, where multiple pieces of data are combined into a single response, can reduce the number of requests and speed up the overall experience.

Caching is a powerful method for enhancing API performance. By storing frequently accessed data in memory, you can reduce the need for repetitive calculations or database queries. Implementing caching strategies at various levels—such as server-side, client-side, or through a dedicated caching layer—can dramatically improve response times and reduce load on your backend systems.

In addition to caching, consider using asynchronous processing for resource-intensive operations. By offloading heavy tasks to background workers, your API can quickly respond to requests while processing demanding operations separately. This approach not only improves response times but also enhances scalability, allowing your application to handle a larger number of concurrent users.

Another performance optimization technique is to minimize the size of API responses. This can be achieved through data compression, reducing the amount of data transmitted over the network. Additionally, consider implementing pagination for endpoints that return large datasets. By providing smaller, manageable chunks of data, you can improve response times and reduce memory usage on both the server and client sides.

Finally, regularly monitoring and profiling your API's performance is essential for identifying areas that require improvement. Tools like API analytics and performance monitoring services can provide valuable insights into response times, error rates, and usage patterns. By continuously evaluating and optimizing your API, you can ensure it meets user expectations and performs efficiently over time.

In summary, optimizing API performance is crucial for delivering a seamless user experience. By focusing on response times, request minimization, caching, asynchronous processing, response size, and ongoing monitoring, you can enhance the overall performance of your API and support the long-term success of your application.

Techniques for improving API response times

Improving API response times is vital for providing a better user experience and maintaining the efficiency of your application. Several techniques can be employed to enhance response times, ranging from optimizing backend processes to implementing caching strategies. Here are some effective methods for achieving faster API responses.

Database optimization: Slow database queries are often the primary culprits behind sluggish API performance. To optimize database interactions, start by analyzing query performance and ensuring that indexes are correctly applied to relevant fields. Additionally, consider using query optimization techniques such as reducing the number of joins, avoiding subqueries where possible, and fetching only the necessary fields.

Data caching: Implementing caching mechanisms can significantly improve response times by storing frequently accessed data in memory. Use in-memory caching solutions like Redis or Memcached to cache API responses or specific database queries. By serving cached data instead of querying the database repeatedly, you can reduce latency and enhance performance.

Load balancing: Distributing incoming requests across multiple servers can help manage traffic and improve response times. Load balancers can efficiently route requests to available servers, ensuring that no single server becomes overwhelmed. This technique not only improves response times but also enhances the overall reliability and availability of your API.

Asynchronous processing: For resource-intensive operations, consider using asynchronous processing to handle tasks in the background. By offloading heavy computations or external API calls to background workers, your API can return responses quickly while processing demanding tasks separately. This approach is especially beneficial for tasks such as sending emails or processing large datasets.

Reduce payload size: Minimizing the size of API responses can lead to faster transmission times. Techniques such as data compression (e.g., Gzip) can help reduce response size. Additionally, consider using more efficient data formats, such as Protocol Buffers or MessagePack, which can serialize data more compactly than JSON or XML.

Pagination and filtering: For endpoints that return large datasets, implement pagination and filtering to limit the amount of data returned in a single response. By breaking down large datasets into smaller chunks, you can improve response times and reduce memory usage. This technique not only enhances performance but also provides a better experience for users who may not need to load all available data at once.

Content Delivery Networks (CDNs): For APIs that serve static content (like images or files), consider using a CDN to cache and deliver content closer to users. CDNs distribute content across multiple servers around the globe, reducing latency and speeding up access for users in different geographical locations.

Optimize API design: Review your API endpoints and design to ensure they are efficient. Use RESTful principles to keep your API intuitive and minimize the number of requests needed to obtain data. Group related resources in a single endpoint to reduce the number of requests and improve response times.

By implementing these techniques, you can effectively improve your API's response times and provide a better user experience. Regularly monitoring and profiling your API will help you identify performance bottlenecks and continually optimize your application's performance.

caching strategies for APIs

Caching is a powerful technique for improving API performance by storing frequently accessed data, which reduces the need for repeated processing and database queries. By effectively implementing caching strategies, you can enhance response times, reduce server load, and optimize resource utilization. Here are some common caching strategies for APIs:

In-memory caching: This involves storing data in memory for quick access. Solutions like Redis or Memcached are popular choices for in-memory caching, allowing you to cache API responses or specific database queries. In-memory caching is particularly effective for data that doesn't change frequently and can dramatically improve response times.

HTTP caching: Leveraging HTTP caching headers allows clients and intermediaries (like CDNs) to cache responses based on specified rules. By using headers like

Cache-Control, Expires, and ETag, you can control how long responses should be cached, whether they can be shared among clients, and when they should be considered stale. This approach reduces server load and speeds up response times for cached requests.

Client-side caching: Encourage clients to cache responses locally to reduce the number of requests made to your API. By including appropriate caching headers, you can instruct clients to store responses temporarily, allowing them to serve cached data for subsequent requests. This is especially useful for static data that doesn't change often.

Database query caching: If your API relies heavily on database queries, consider implementing caching for frequently executed queries. By caching query results, you can reduce the load on the database and improve response times. Tools like Django's built-in caching framework or SQL query caching in your database can help implement this strategy.

Content Delivery Networks (CDNs): For APIs that serve static content (e.g., images, scripts), using a CDN can cache and deliver content from edge servers closer to users. This not only speeds up access to static resources but also offloads traffic from your main servers, improving overall API performance.

Cache invalidation: An essential aspect of caching is ensuring that cached data remains accurate and up-to-date. Implement cache invalidation strategies to determine when cached data should be refreshed. Common methods include time-based expiration (where cached data is invalidated after a specific period) or event-based invalidation (where changes in the underlying data trigger cache refreshes).

Layered caching: Consider implementing multiple caching layers to optimize performance further. For example, you might use a combination of in-memory caching for frequently accessed data, HTTP caching for static responses, and database query caching to handle complex queries efficiently. Layered caching allows you to maximize the benefits of each caching strategy.

By employing these caching strategies, you can significantly improve the performance of your API, leading to faster response times and a better user experience. Regularly evaluate and optimize your caching implementation to ensure it aligns with your application's needs and user expectations.

Monitoring and profiling API performance

Monitoring and profiling your API performance is crucial for identifying bottlenecks, optimizing response times, and ensuring a seamless user experience. By actively tracking key performance metrics, you can gain insights into how your API is functioning and make informed decisions to improve its efficiency. Here are some essential practices for effectively monitoring and profiling API performance:

Establish performance metrics: Define key performance indicators (KPIs) to monitor your API's health. Common metrics include response times, error rates, throughput (requests per second), and latency. Establishing benchmarks for these metrics will help you gauge the performance of your API over time.

Implement logging: Logging is vital for tracking API requests and responses. By capturing detailed logs of API interactions, you can identify trends, diagnose issues, and analyze user behavior. Use structured logging formats (like JSON) to facilitate easier querying and analysis of log data.

Use monitoring tools: Leverage monitoring tools and services to gain real-time insights into your API's performance. Solutions like New Relic, Datadog, or Prometheus can help you visualize metrics, set alerts for abnormal behavior, and monitor resource usage. These tools often provide dashboards to track performance over time and facilitate comparison against established benchmarks.

Conduct load testing: Regularly conduct load tests to simulate traffic and evaluate how your API performs under different conditions. Tools like Apache JMeter or Locust can help you create and run load tests, providing insights into how your API handles increased

Chapter 15

Securing your APIs

Importance of API security

Securing your APIs is critical in today's digital landscape, where data breaches and cyber threats are increasingly common. APIs often serve as gateways to sensitive data and functionality, making them prime targets for malicious actors. Implementing robust security measures helps protect your application, safeguard user information, and maintain the integrity of your services. A security breach can lead to reputational damage, financial loss, and legal consequences, so prioritizing API security is essential for any organization.

One fundamental aspect of API security is authentication. Ensuring that only authorized users can access your API is crucial. Common methods include API keys, OAuth, and JSON Web Tokens (JWTs). These authentication mechanisms help verify the identity of users and applications interacting with your API, ensuring that only legitimate requests are processed.

In addition to authentication, authorization is another key component. Once a user is authenticated, it's vital to determine what actions they are permitted to perform.

Implementing role-based access control (RBAC) or attribute-based access control (ABAC) allows you to enforce granular permissions, ensuring that users can only access resources they are authorized to use.

Data encryption is another critical security measure. Encrypting data in transit (using HTTPS) protects sensitive information from being intercepted during transmission. Additionally, consider encrypting data at rest to safeguard it from unauthorized access or breaches. Using strong encryption algorithms helps ensure the confidentiality and integrity of your data.

Rate limiting is a useful technique for preventing abuse of your API. By setting limits on the number of requests a user or application can make within a specific timeframe, you can mitigate the risk of denial-of-service (DoS) attacks and protect your API from excessive load. Rate limiting helps ensure fair usage and can improve the overall stability of your API.

Regular security assessments and vulnerability testing are essential for identifying and addressing potential weaknesses in your API. Conduct penetration testing, code reviews, and security audits to uncover vulnerabilities and ensure compliance with security standards. Staying informed about the latest security threats and best practices will help you proactively safeguard your API against emerging risks.

Finally, maintain clear and comprehensive documentation of your security practices. This includes guidelines for authentication, authorization, and secure coding practices. Educating your development team on security best practices fosters a security-minded culture within your organization, reducing the likelihood of vulnerabilities arising from common coding mistakes.

In summary, API security is a critical aspect of application development that should not be overlooked. By focusing on authentication, authorization, data encryption, rate limiting, security assessments, and clear documentation, you can significantly enhance the security posture of your APIs and protect your organization against potential threats.

Common vulnerabilities and how to mitigate them

APIs can be vulnerable to various security threats that may compromise data integrity, confidentiality, and availability. Understanding these vulnerabilities and implementing effective mitigation strategies is essential for securing your APIs. Here are some common vulnerabilities and ways to address them:

Injection attacks: Injection attacks, such as SQL injection and command injection, occur when untrusted data is executed as code. To mitigate this risk, always validate and sanitize user input, use parameterized queries for database access, and employ ORM frameworks to prevent direct interaction with the database.

Cross-Site Scripting (XSS): XSS attacks involve injecting malicious scripts into web applications that are then executed by unsuspecting users. To prevent XSS, validate and escape user input, employ content security policies (CSP), and use libraries that automatically handle encoding for you.

Insecure authentication: Weak or poorly implemented authentication mechanisms can allow unauthorized access to your API. Use strong authentication methods, such as OAuth 2.0 or JWT, and implement multi-factor authentication (MFA) where possible. Regularly rotate API keys and enforce strong password policies.

Improper authorization: Insufficient authorization checks can lead to users accessing resources they shouldn't. Implement strict access control policies and always validate permissions on the server side. Use RBAC or ABAC to ensure users can only perform actions they are authorized to do.

Sensitive data exposure: Failing to protect sensitive data can lead to breaches. Always use HTTPS to encrypt data in transit and consider encrypting sensitive data at rest. Avoid exposing sensitive information in API responses and use proper data masking techniques.

Rate limiting and throttling: Without rate limiting, APIs are susceptible to abuse and denial-of-service attacks. Implement rate limiting to control the number of requests a user can make within a specific time frame. This helps prevent abuse and ensures fair usage.

Misconfigured CORS (Cross-Origin Resource Sharing): Improperly configured CORS can expose your API to unauthorized domains. Ensure that CORS policies are strictly defined and only allow trusted origins to access your API.

Lack of logging and monitoring: Insufficient logging can hinder your ability to detect and respond to security incidents. Implement comprehensive logging and monitoring to track API usage, identify unusual patterns, and respond promptly to potential threats.

By being aware of these common vulnerabilities and taking proactive measures to mitigate them, you can significantly enhance the security of your APIs. Regularly reviewing and updating your security practices is essential to keep pace with evolving threats and ensure the ongoing protection of your application and user data.

Best practices for securing APIs

Securing your APIs requires a comprehensive approach that encompasses various best practices. By implementing these strategies, you can significantly reduce the risk of vulnerabilities and protect sensitive data. Here are some best practices for securing APIs:

Use HTTPS: Always encrypt data in transit by using HTTPS. This ensures that data exchanged between clients and your API remains confidential and is protected from interception. Enforcing HTTPS not only secures your API but also enhances user trust.

Implement strong authentication and authorization: Use robust authentication mechanisms, such as OAuth 2.0, JWTs, or API keys. Ensure that you also enforce strict authorization policies to control access to resources. Implement RBAC or ABAC to define permissions clearly and prevent unauthorized actions.

Validate and sanitize user input: Always validate and sanitize incoming data to prevent injection attacks and data corruption. Use input validation libraries and ensure that data adheres to expected formats before processing it.

Limit data exposure: Be cautious about the data returned in API responses. Avoid exposing sensitive information and use proper data masking techniques. Implement pagination for large datasets and provide only the necessary information to users.

Implement rate limiting: Control the number of requests that users can make to your API within a specified timeframe. Rate limiting helps prevent abuse, mitigates denial-of-service attacks, and ensures fair resource usage.

Regularly update and patch: Keep your API and its dependencies updated to address security vulnerabilities. Regularly review your codebase and third-party libraries to ensure they are patched and up to date.

Conduct security assessments: Regularly perform security audits, penetration testing, and vulnerability assessments to identify and address potential weaknesses. Continuous evaluation helps you stay ahead of emerging threats.

Monitor and log API activity: Implement comprehensive logging to track API usage and monitor for unusual patterns or potential security incidents. Use monitoring tools to gain insights into performance and security metrics.

Educate your team: Foster a security-minded culture within your development team. Provide training on secure coding practices and the importance of API security to reduce the likelihood of introducing vulnerabilities.

Document security practices: Maintain clear documentation of your API security practices, including authentication methods, authorization policies, and security protocols. This transparency helps users understand how to interact with your API securely.

By following these best practices, you can significantly enhance the security of your APIs and protect your application and user data from potential threats. Regularly revisiting and updating these practices is essential to adapt to the ever-evolving landscape of security challenges.

Chapter 16

Consuming RESTful APIs in Python

Overview of API clients

API clients are essential tools that allow developers to interact with RESTful APIs. They serve as intermediaries, enabling communication between applications and web services by sending requests to APIs and processing the responses received. In Python, several libraries facilitate the creation of API clients, simplifying the process of consuming RESTful services. Understanding how these clients work and the various libraries available can greatly enhance your ability to integrate with different APIs.

An API client typically follows a straightforward workflow: it constructs an HTTP request, sends it to the API endpoint, and then receives and processes the response. The request may include parameters, headers, and a body, depending on the API's specifications. Once the response is received, the client can parse the data, handle errors, and return results in a usable format.

In Python, the most commonly used library for making HTTP requests is requests. This library provides a simple and intuitive interface for sending HTTP requests, making it easy to work with various types of APIs. With requests, developers can handle GET, POST, PUT, DELETE, and other HTTP methods without delving into the complexities of raw HTTP communication.

In addition to requests, Python offers other libraries such as httpx, which supports asynchronous requests and provides a more modern approach to handling HTTP. There are also specialized libraries like aiohttp, which is designed for asynchronous programming and allows for efficient handling of concurrent requests.

When building an API client, it's important to handle various scenarios effectively. This includes managing authentication, parsing responses, and handling errors gracefully. A well-designed API client should abstract away the complexity of these tasks, providing developers with a straightforward interface for interacting with the API.

Moreover, while consuming APIs, developers should also consider factors such as rate limiting and pagination. Many APIs impose limits on the number of requests that can be made within a certain timeframe. API clients should be designed to respect these limits and implement strategies to handle pagination when dealing with large datasets. This ensures that the application remains compliant with API usage policies and provides a seamless user experience.

In summary, API clients are crucial for interacting with RESTful APIs in Python. Understanding the available libraries, the workflow of making requests, and handling responses and errors is essential for effective API consumption. By leveraging tools like requests and adhering to best practices, developers can build robust applications that integrate seamlessly with external services.

using requests library to consume APIs

The requests library is the most popular choice among Python developers for consuming RESTful APIs due to its simplicity and ease of use. It provides a straightforward way to send HTTP requests, handle responses, and manage parameters. Below, we'll explore how to utilize the requests library to interact with APIs effectively.

To begin using requests, you first need to install it if you haven't already. You can install the library via pip:

```bash
Copy code
pip install requests
```

Once installed, you can start making requests to an API. The most basic usage involves sending a GET request to retrieve data from an API endpoint. Here's an example of how to do this:

```python
Copy code
import requests

response = requests.get('https://api.example.com/data')

if response.status_code == 200:
data = response.json()
print(data)
else:
print(f"Error: {response.status_code}")
```

In this example, we send a GET request to the specified URL and check the response status code. If the request is successful (status code 200), we parse the JSON response using the .json() method, which automatically converts the JSON data into a Python dictionary.

When consuming APIs, you often need to send additional parameters or headers with your requests. The requests library makes this easy. For example, to send query parameters with a GET request, you can do the following:

python
Copy code

```
params = {'key': 'value', 'another_key': 'another_value'}
response = requests.get('https://api.example.com/data',
params=params)
```

If you need to send data in the body of a request, such as in a POST request, you can do this by specifying the data or json argument:

python
Copy code

```
data = {'name': 'John', 'age': 30}
response = requests.post('https://api.example.com/users',
json=data)
```

This sends a JSON payload to the specified endpoint, and the server can process the data accordingly. Similarly, if you need to send form-encoded data, you can use the data parameter instead:

python
Copy code

```
form_data = {'username': 'user', 'password': 'pass'}
response = requests.post('https://api.example.com/login',
data=form_data)
```

Authentication is another critical aspect of consuming APIs. Many APIs require you to authenticate your requests using API keys or tokens. You can include these credentials in the headers:

python
Copy code
```
headers = {'Authorization': 'Bearer YOUR_API_TOKEN'}
response = requests.get('https://api.example.com/protected', headers=headers)
```

Handling errors is also crucial when consuming APIs. The requests library provides built-in mechanisms for checking response status codes and handling exceptions. You can raise exceptions for HTTP errors using the raise_for_status() method:

python
Copy code
```
try:
response.raise_for_status()
data = response.json()
except requests.exceptions.HTTPError as err:
print(f"HTTP error occurred: {err}")
```

In addition to basic GET and POST requests, the requests library also supports other HTTP methods like PUT and DELETE, enabling full CRUD (Create, Read, Update, Delete) operations on RESTful APIs:

python
Copy code
```
# PUT request to update data
update_data = {'name': 'Jane'}
response = requests.put('https://api.example.com/users/1',
json=update_data)

# DELETE request to remove data
response                                              =
requests.delete('https://api.example.com/users/1')
```

In summary, the requests library simplifies the process of consuming RESTful APIs in Python. By providing intuitive methods for making HTTP requests, handling parameters and headers, and managing responses, it enables developers to integrate with APIs efficiently. By following best practices and understanding error handling, you can build robust applications that leverage the power of external services.

Handling JSON responses and errors

When consuming RESTful APIs, handling JSON responses and errors effectively is crucial for building resilient applications. JSON is the most common format for data interchange in APIs, and understanding how to parse and utilize this data is key to successful integration. Additionally, robust error handling is essential to ensure that your application can gracefully handle unexpected situations.

After sending a request to an API using the requests library, the response is typically in JSON format. You can easily parse this response into a Python dictionary using the .json() method, as demonstrated earlier. Here's a quick reminder of how to do this:

```python
Copy code
response = requests.get('https://api.example.com/data')

if response.status_code == 200:
data = response.json()
print(data)
```

In this example, we check if the response status code is 200 (indicating success) before attempting to parse the JSON data. If the response is successful, you can then work with the data as needed.

However, APIs may return different status codes based on the outcome of your request. It's important to handle these codes appropriately to provide meaningful feedback to the user or to trigger specific actions in your application. For instance, if a request fails due to a client error (status codes 400–499), you might want to log the error or alert the user.

Here's how you can structure your error handling:

python
Copy code

```
response = requests.get('https://api.example.com/data')

try:
response.raise_for_status()  # Raises an error for HTTP errors
data = response.json()
# Process data here
except requests.exceptions.HTTPError as http_err:
print(f"HTTP error occurred: {http_err}")
except requests.exceptions.RequestException as err:
print(f"Error occurred: {err}")
```

In this example, raise_for_status() will raise an exception for any HTTP error responses, allowing you to handle them in a structured manner. You can catch specific exceptions like HTTPError to respond differently based on the type of error. Additionally, you can catch RequestException to handle any other issues related to the request.

Some APIs also provide detailed error messages in their JSON responses. These messages can be useful for debugging and user feedback. For instance, a typical error response might look like this:

json
Copy code

```json
{
"error": {
"code": 404,
"message": "Resource not found"
}
}
```

You can access this information by parsing the JSON response even in the case of an error:

python
Copy code

```python
response = requests.get('https://api.example.com/resource/unknown')

if response.status_code != 200:
```

```python
error_info = response.json().get('error', {})
print(f"Error                        {error_info.get('code')}:
{error_info.get('message')}")
```

This approach allows you to provide meaningful feedback based on the specific error returned by the API, improving the user experience.

In some cases, you may encounter rate limiting errors, where the API informs you that you've exceeded the allowed number of requests. These responses often include headers indicating when you can make your next request. Be sure to check for headers like Retry-After to implement appropriate waiting logic in your application:

python
Copy code

```python
if response.status_code == 429:  # Too Many Requests
retry_after = int(response.headers.get('Retry-After', 0))
print(f"Rate limit exceeded. Retry after {retry_after}
seconds.")
```

By implementing robust error handling and properly parsing JSON responses, you can build a more resilient API client that gracefully manages unexpected situations and provides a better experience for users.

Chapter 17

Deploying your API

Overview of deployment options

Deploying an API is a critical step in the application development lifecycle, transforming your code from a local environment into a fully operational service accessible to users. There are several deployment options available, each with its own advantages and considerations. Understanding these options will help you choose the best fit for your API's needs, performance requirements, and budget constraints.

One of the most popular deployment options is using cloud platforms such as **Heroku, AWS,** and **DigitalOcean**. These platforms provide managed services that simplify the deployment process and offer scalability, reliability, and various tools for monitoring and managing your applications.

Heroku is known for its simplicity and developer-friendly environment. It allows you to deploy applications with just a few commands using Git. Heroku abstracts much of the underlying infrastructure management, enabling developers to focus on writing code. It also offers add-ons for databases, caching, and monitoring, which can be easily integrated into your application. Heroku's free tier allows for quick testing and development but may have limitations in terms of performance and uptime.

AWS (Amazon Web Services) is a more robust and scalable solution. It provides a wide range of services, including Elastic Beanstalk for easy deployment of applications, Lambda for serverless architecture, and EC2 for full control over virtual servers. While AWS offers greater flexibility and scalability, it can be more complex to set up and manage. Understanding AWS services requires a steeper learning curve, but it also provides powerful features for monitoring, security, and resource management.

DigitalOcean is another cloud provider that offers a balance between simplicity and power. With its Droplets (virtual machines), you can quickly set up your API with full control over the operating system and environment. DigitalOcean also provides managed database services, Kubernetes for container orchestration, and Spaces for object storage. It is often favored by startups and smaller teams due to its straightforward pricing and user-friendly interface.

When deploying your API, consider whether you prefer a **Platform as a Service (PaaS)** or **Infrastructure as a Service (IaaS)** approach. PaaS providers like Heroku and

AWS Elastic Beanstalk manage the underlying infrastructure, allowing you to focus on your code. In contrast, IaaS providers like AWS EC2 or DigitalOcean Droplets give you more control over the environment but require more management and configuration.

Another important factor in deployment is **containerization**. Using technologies like Docker, you can package your application along with its dependencies into a single container. This approach ensures consistency across different environments and simplifies deployment. Kubernetes, a container orchestration tool, can help manage and scale your containerized applications, providing high availability and efficient resource management.

In addition to cloud platforms and containerization, consider your API's **versioning** and **monitoring** requirements. Implementing versioning strategies ensures backward compatibility and allows you to make changes without disrupting existing users. Monitoring tools, such as Prometheus or Grafana, help you track API performance and identify issues in real time, ensuring a smooth experience for your users.

In summary, the deployment of your API involves selecting the right platform and strategy to meet your application's needs. Consider factors such as ease of use, scalability, control, and monitoring when choosing between cloud platforms like Heroku, AWS, and DigitalOcean. Embracing containerization can also enhance the consistency and reliability of your deployments.

Preparing your Flask and Django applications for production

Preparing your Flask or Django application for production involves several crucial steps to ensure that your API is secure, performant, and ready for real-world usage. Both frameworks have their specific requirements and best practices, but some common themes emerge when moving from a development environment to production.

First and foremost, you need to configure your application settings for production. This includes setting the DEBUG mode to False in Django, which prevents the exposure of sensitive debugging information in case of errors. In Flask, ensure that you set the application's environment to production:

```python
Copy code
app.config['ENV'] = 'production'
```

For both frameworks, it is essential to manage your secret keys and sensitive data properly. Avoid hardcoding secrets in your source code. Instead, use environment variables or secret management tools to store sensitive information securely. Tools like python-decouple or dotenv can help manage configuration settings without compromising security.

Next, consider your database configuration. In a production environment, you should use a robust database management system, such as PostgreSQL or MySQL, rather than the lightweight SQLite used during development. Ensure that you configure your database connection settings properly and apply any necessary migrations before deploying.

For both Flask and Django, you need to set up a production-ready web server. Development servers, such as Django's built-in server or Flask's development server, are not suitable for production due to performance and security issues. Instead, use a WSGI server like **Gunicorn** or **uWSGI** to serve your application. For instance, to run a Flask app with Gunicorn, you would use:

bash
Copy code
```
gunicorn -w 4 myapp:app
```

This command runs the application with 4 worker processes, allowing it to handle multiple requests concurrently.

Setting up a reverse proxy server, like **Nginx** or **Apache**, is also essential for production deployments. The reverse proxy can manage incoming requests, handle SSL termination, and provide additional security features. For example, Nginx can serve static files directly and forward requests to your WSGI server:

nginx
Copy code
```
server {
listen 80;
server_name example.com;

location / {
proxy_pass http://localhost:8000;
}

location /static/ {
alias /path/to/static/files/;
}
}
```

SSL certificates are critical for securing your API. Use **Let's Encrypt** to obtain free SSL certificates and configure your web server to enforce HTTPS. This protects data in transit and enhances user trust in your application.

Additionally, consider implementing logging and error tracking in your production environment. Use libraries like **Sentry** or **Loggly** to capture and monitor errors, helping you diagnose issues quickly. Ensure that your application logs important events and errors to provide insight into its operation.

Monitoring your application's performance is crucial for maintaining a smooth user experience. Implement tools like **Prometheus** or **Grafana** to track key performance metrics, including response times, error rates, and system resource usage. Regularly review these metrics to identify bottlenecks and optimize your API's performance.

Finally, be prepared for scaling your application. As usage grows, you may need to scale vertically (upgrading your server resources) or horizontally (adding more instances). Using container orchestration tools like **Kubernetes** can help manage scaling and resource allocation efficiently.

In conclusion, preparing your Flask or Django application for production involves configuring settings, managing secrets, setting up a robust web server, enforcing security measures, implementing logging and monitoring, and planning for scalability. By following these best practices, you can ensure that your API operates effectively in a production environment.

Setting up a production database and environment variables

Setting up a production database and managing environment variables are crucial steps in deploying a secure and reliable API. A well-configured database and proper management of environment variables ensure that your application operates efficiently and securely in a production environment.

When selecting a database for your production API, consider the specific requirements of your application. Popular choices include relational databases like PostgreSQL and MySQL, or NoSQL databases like MongoDB, depending on your data structure and access patterns. For most applications, a relational database provides robust features, including ACID compliance, which ensures data integrity and reliability.

To set up a production database, start by provisioning the database server on your chosen platform, whether it's a cloud provider or on-premise hardware. For example, if you're using AWS, you can use **Amazon RDS** (Relational Database Service) to create and manage a PostgreSQL or MySQL database instance. This service handles backups, scaling, and high availability for you, simplifying database management.

Once the database instance is set up, you need to configure your application to connect to it. In both Flask and Django, this involves specifying connection settings such as the database host, port, username, password, and database name. For security reasons, avoid hardcoding these values in your source code. Instead, store them in environment variables.

In a Django application, you can configure your database settings in the settings.py file. For example:

```python
Copy code
import os

DATABASES = {
'default': {
'ENGINE': 'django.db.backends.postgresql',
'NAME': os.environ.get('DB_NAME'),
'USER': os.environ.get('DB_USER'),
'PASSWORD': os.environ.get('DB_PASSWORD'),
'HOST': os.environ.get('DB_HOST'),
'PORT': os.environ.get('DB_PORT', '5432'),
}
}
```

In this example, os.environ.get is used to retrieve database credentials from environment variables, ensuring that sensitive information is not exposed in the codebase.

For Flask, you can similarly configure the database connection using environment variables in your application configuration:

```python
Copy code
import os

app.config['SQLALCHEMY_DATABASE_URI'] = f"postgresql://{os.environ.get('DB_USER')}:{os.environ.get('DB_PASSWORD')}@{os.environ.get('DB_HOST')}:{os.environ.get('DB_PORT')}/{os.environ.get('DB_NAME')}"
```

To manage environment variables effectively, consider using tools like python-decouple, dotenv, or built-in capabilities provided by cloud platforms. For instance, AWS allows you to store environment variables securely using **AWS Systems Manager Parameter Store** or **AWS Secrets Manager**. This helps keep your application configuration secure and manageable.

Once your application is configured to connect to the production database, it's time to migrate your database schema. In Django, you can run the following command to apply migrations.

www.ingramcontent.com/pod-product-compliance
Lightning Source LLC
LaVergne TN
LVHW051336050326
832903LV00031B/3574